Father Gallwey

The Precious Pearl of Hope in the Mercy of God

Answers to Certain Difficulties which are a Hindrance to Hope

Father Gallwey

The Precious Pearl of Hope in the Mercy of God
Answers to Certain Difficulties which are a Hindrance to Hope

ISBN/EAN: 9783741197932

Manufactured in Europe, USA, Canada, Australia, Japa

Cover: Foto ©Lupo / pixelio.de

Manufactured and distributed by brebook publishing software (www.brebook.com)

Father Gallwey

The Precious Pearl of Hope in the Mercy of God

THE PRECIOUS PEARL OF HOPE IN THE MERCY OF GOD.

ANSWERS TO CERTAIN DIFFICULTIES WHICH ARE A HINDRANCE TO HOPE.

TRANSLATED FROM THE ITALIAN BY

K. G.

With a Preface by

FATHER GALLWEY, S.J.

LONDON: BURNS AND OATES.

—

1878.

PREFACE.

THIS little volume contains only Part II. of the Italian work, *Tesori di Confidenza in Dio*. The first part has not been translated, because, though full of piety and holy thoughts, it does not differ much from other works already extant in our language, and would therefore not be so useful an addition to our ascetical literature as, it is hoped, this second part will prove. Every treatise that helps to keep alive in our soul the Divine gift of hope deserves to be called a precious treasure, since, though the Psalmist exhorts us to hope in the Lord from the morning watch even until night, yet, on the other hand, the enemy of God labours incessantly night and day to propagate amongst us false ideas concerning our God, and above all the blasphemous calumny that He is not infinitely merciful and compassionate. We require therefore to be reminded very often of the truth that He has revealed concerning His compassion for us; how untiring is His patience with us; how ready He always is, nay, how He yearns with desire to forgive all our sins, be they red as scarlet, and numerous as the hairs of our head. The father of lies has never completely gained his point, never achieved the triumph for which he longs, till he has induced us to accept the lie that our God is not any longer a Father to us, and that the Passion and death of our Saviour are not sufficient to obtain mercy for our case. We do not perceive when despairing thus that, while we seem to be only depreciating ourselves and owning the heinousness of our sins, we are all the while rejecting the great truth which God has revealed concerning Himself—that His mercy is above all His works, and that for His own sake and for His Name's sake He delights in showing mercy. Hence holy men advise us to make acts of hope in this form—"For Thy sake, my God, I hope in Thee." That is to say—"Knowing that, like a good Father, Thou art well pleased that I should hope in Thee, and knowing too that the devils are much displeased and confounded when I give Thee honour by professing aloud that Thou art a merciful and compassionate God, and by putting my trust in Thee, I do, in spite of my great unworthiness and my many sins, firmly hope in Thy mercy, which is greater than my unworthiness, and in the multitude of Thy mercies, which outnumber all my sins."

Preface. vii

Speaking in his book on penance of the sin of Judas, St. Augustine has these words—"It was not the crime which he had committed which completed the ruin of Judas, but his despair of pardon;" and then he goes on to explain how despair works upon the soul, by saying that what Judas did to his body was an image of what he did to his soul; for as the halter around the neck prevents the air of this world from entering into the body, so despair of God's mercy chokes the soul and hinders the Holy Ghost from finding an entrance into it.

Again and again, then, let us accustom our souls to acts of hope, turning away from the spectacle of our miseries to the spectacle of God's unbounded mercy, and saying, with the pious and learned Father Lessius —"Truly Thou art God, and of Thy mercies there is no number, and of Thy goodness the store is infinite! O Lord, who is like to Thee! For even when judging Thou art still a Father, and ready to forgive the ten thousand talents if Thou but hear the pitiful cry— 'Have patience with me and I will repay all.' Nay, for the sake of that one word, *Peccavi*—'I have sinned,' uttered by a truly contrite heart, Thou dost forgive ten thousand times a hundred thousand deadly sins. O Lord, who is like to Thee!"

Under the protection then of her who is called the

Mother of holy hope, this volume is sent forth that it may, along with the admirable chapter against Despair in Father Parsons' *Christian Directory*, Father Rogacci's excellent treatise on Holy Confidence, and other similar works, help many to keep holy hope alive in their hearts, "from the morning watch even until night," through all the vicissitudes of this ever changing life.

PETER GALLWEY, S.J.

Feb. 18th, 1878.

AUTHOR'S PREFACE.

THE first part of this compendium contains a connected enumeration of the strongest motives for awakening in us an absolute confidence in God. These motives ought to be more than sufficient, both to remove all obstacles in the way of the sinner's rapid conversion, and to kindle in all the liveliest desire to grow rich in merit, seeing the inestimable treasures God has placed in our hands. As, however, there occur in Scripture some passages which give occasion for the sophisms of unbelievers and heretics, and have no small tendency to make the faithful themselves lose heart in the service of God, it seemed necessary to add this second part, explanatory of the texts in question, with a view to facilitate the attainment of the two-fold object above-mentioned.

In former times some of the Scripture texts had, by an abuse of the letter, been wrested by heresiarchs to a furtherance of their errors; but these heretics having been condemned by the Catholic Church, and their interpretation of these texts of Scripture having been universally admitted to be heretical, all men were on their guard against the errors thus condemned. Under these circumstances, therefore, many Catholic writers did not hesitate to avail themselves of the texts in question to inspire the faithful with a wholesome fear, taking care, however, always to use them in the sense approved by the Church. And as the faith was deeply rooted in the hearts of their readers, there was no danger that hope would grow less, or an odious idea of God be introduced as a consequence of their writings. But a time having arrived when faith has become cold and love almost worn out—a time when Christians seem prone to diffidence and averse to the service of God—a time more especially when unbelievers are beginning to swarm, and their books, wherein many of the texts in question are treated as opposed to reason and common sense, are read with avidity—a time when the inspiration of Scripture is denied, and Atheism or Deism covertly taught—it has seemed to the chief champions of religion, such as Bergier and Nonnotte, a matter of duty thoroughly to examine and fully to explain the true sense of these texts, tested by the rules of the severest criticism, the tradition of the Fathers, and the spirit of the Catholic Church.

Accordingly in this second part the difficulties started by unbelievers, as well as those occurring to the faithful themselves whose courage fails in the presence of mistrust, are treated of, and the sense of the above-mentioned texts is carefully investigated under the guidance of the Apologists before referred to, and of those who interpret the Holy Scriptures after the spirit of the Catholic Church. The true sense is therein shown to be not only opposed to the interpretation put forth by unbelievers, heretics, and innovators, but far removed from any injurious fear or discouragement for souls that are anxious to work out their salvation, and give themselves wholly to God.

CONTENTS.

	PAGE
PREFACE	v
AUTHOR'S PREFACE	ix

Chapter I.—Does the Christian Religion inspire terror and discouragement? 1
Chapter II.—Whether moral certainty of being in a state of grace, and of the pardon of sin, is attainable in the Christian religion 10
Chapter III.—The meaning to be attached to the phrase, "the hardness and blindness of sinners" . . . 29
Chapter IV.—On the sense in which we are to understand God's abandonment of sinners, and their reprobation . 50
Chapter V.—On lukewarmness 69
Chapter VI.—On relapse into sin 75
Chapter VII.—On the number of the chosen . . . 85
Chapter VIII.—Discussion of the question whether, with God's assistance, salvation is of easy or difficult attainment 136
Chapter IX.—Discussion of the question whether the justice of God is not another name for severity . . . 151
Chapter X.—Discussion of the question whether the generality of preachers and ascetic writers concur in the foregoing interpretation of the texts herein selected for exposition . 183
Chapter XI.—Question considered: Is the method of directing souls by the way of confidence a dangerous one? . . 189

THE PRECIOUS PEARL OF HOPE IN GOD.

SOLUTION OF DIFFICULTIES AGAINST HOPE.

CHAPTER I.

Does the Christian religion inspire terror and discouragement?

FIRST DIFFICULTY.—How can any one serve God in peace and tranquillity, if religion itself fills its unhappy followers with the greatest fear and terror by its oft-repeated threats of eternal fire and the most dreadful torments?

Surely a religion, in order to be worthy of God, should also be congenial to the heart of man, who is to profess it, and thus inspire him with love and confidence towards his Creator. Therefore the Christian religion cannot be considered true or worthy of God.[1]

Answer.—The Christian religion, answers Bergier, founded on the charity of its Divine Author, Who is essentially infinite goodness, inspires with terror and fear, not its faithful followers, but only him who refuses to profess it in order to live according to his passions; and it strives by its very threats to make the erring

---

[1] Bergier, *Traité de la vraie Religion*, refutes these and similar objections taken from the impious authors of *Le Chrétien devoilé* and *Le tableau des Saints*, &c.

enter into themselves for their own good, in order that they may escape eternal evils.

It is true, therefore, that, as malefactors in civil society threatened with the severest punishments of the law for their crimes have reason to fear, so also have those obstinate sinners reason to fear who only bear the name of Christian to dishonour it by professing irreligious opinions, or by leading a life entirely contrary to the precepts and teaching of the Catholic religion. On the other hand, as good citizens find no cause for uneasiness in laws against crime, but would rather see reason for apprehension if there were no laws existing, since the chief end of such laws is the prevention of crime and consequently the peace and security of society; so in like manner still less cause have they who desire to live like good Christians for excessive fear, knowing as they do that damnation is not a thing that can come upon us by chance, and that no one is sentenced to Hell who does not voluntarily precipitate himself into it by deliberate and grave transgression of the holy law of God. I said *still less;* because if a good citizen feels no uneasiness with regard to laws against crime, notwithstanding the well-known fact that sometimes the innocent, when falsely accused, are by human laws punished as guilty; how much better reason has a Christian for not being disquieted by the penalties attached to sin, assured as he is of the utter impossibility of God's punishing the innocent. Nay, these very threats of eternal punishment should rather console than sadden the good, since they serve as so many checks and restraints to deter the wicked from indulging in oppression and unjust persecution.

Moreover, the good Christian has a still further security for his mental tranquillity, in his trust in the goodness of God, in the merits of Jesus Christ, in the assistance of His grace, and in His infallible and consoling promises of eternal reward: so that in reality, as Bergier[2] observes, the good Christian who believes in Hell fears much less than the unbeliever who affects to ignore its existence.

Inasmuch, therefore, as the Christian religion threatens the wicked with dreadful punishments in order to restrain them from evil-doing, and promises magnificent rewards to the good in order to encourage them in well-doing, it is for this very reason all the more worthy of God.

SECOND DIFFICULTY.—But how can Christians live in tranquillity and contentment, if their religion commands all without exception *to work out their eternal salvation with fear and trembling?*[3] Or rather is it not clear that this religion which commands at the same time things contradictory, and therefore impossible of accomplishment, is unworthy of a God of infinite wisdom and justice; since in effect His will is that *they serve Him at one and the same time both in fear and in gladness*,[4] as is evident from Scripture texts.

Answer.—In the first place God does not require things contradictory and therefore impossible of accomplishment, because the fear which He particularly desires from His followers is a filial fear, and therefore one not opposed to a holy gladness. "Come, children," says the Royal Prophet, "hearken to me: I will teach you the fear of the Lord."[5] Mark how he calls them children, not servants. He wishes then to inspire them

---

[2] As above, vol. i. p. 61.

[3] "With fear and trembling work out your salvation" (Philipp. ii. 12).

[4] "Serve ye the Lord with fear: and rejoice unto Him with trembling" (Psalm ii. 11). "Serve ye the Lord with gladness" (Psalm xcix. 1).

[5] Psalm xxxiii. 12.

with a fear proper to children, a fear perfectly consistent with gladness; for he informs them that they shall not on account of this fear cease to enjoy life and happy days.[6]

He afterwards teaches them in what this fear consists, namely, in flying from evil and doing good.[7] In this manner, continues the Royal Prophet, "seek peace and pursue it;" that is to say, strive to preserve it at all costs, and never let it be disturbed within you by mistrust; because I will always have My eyes upon you, watchful to guard you, and My ears open to hear your prayers in order to deliver you from all your tribulations;[8] and I will be always near to save you, if you have recourse to Me with humility:[9] in fine, I will have a care of all your bones,[10] and I will redeem your souls, and you shall never be disappointed in the hope you have placed in Me.[11]

The quotation from St. Paul is given here in its entirety for greater clearness:

"Wherefore, my dearly beloved (as you have always obeyed), not as in my presence only, but much more now in my absence *with fear and trembling work out your salvation.* For it is God Who worketh in you,

---

[6] "Who is the man that desireth life: who loveth to see good days?" (Psalm xxxiii. 13).

[7] "Turn away from evil and do good: seek after peace and pursue it" (*Ibid.* v. 15).

[8] "The eyes of the Lord are upon the just: and His ears unto their prayers, . . . and He delivered them out of all their troubles" (*Ibid.* v. 16, 18).

[9] "The Lord is nigh unto them that are of a contrite heart: and He will save the humble of spirit" (*Ibid.* v. 19).

[10] "The Lord keepeth all their bones, not one of them shall be broken" (*Ibid.* v. 21).

[11] "The Lord will redeem the souls of His servants: and none of them that trust in Him shall offend" (*Ibid.* v. 23).

both to will and to accomplish, according to *His* good will." [12]

Bergier [13] infers from this passage that the Apostle, far from wishing to inspire the Philippians with fear, aimed rather at consoling and encouraging them.

He says, in effect, that the Philippians, beset as they were by enemies eager to persecute them, liable at every moment to suffering and conflict, and no longer animated by the presence of St. Paul, were oppressed with fear and trembling, and that the Apostle exhorts them in these critical circumstances to work out their salvation with humility and distrust in themselves, inasmuch as it is God Who by His grace worketh in them to will and to accomplish. We can easily understand this interpretation: but it does not seem conformable with good sense to suppose that the Apostle exhorts the Philippians to fear and tremble because God worketh in them to will and to accomplish *according to His good will*, that is to say, for the love He bears them. His aim is to console, and to encourage them to work out their salvation with humility and mistrust in themselves, in order that they may take the necessary precautions to avoid falling into sin; and he assures them at the same time that God on His side will, *by reason of His good will*, give them the necessary strength and grace. [14]

Mgr. Martini [15] and the best advocates of religion, in

---

[12] "Itaque charissimi (sicut semper obedistis) non ut in præsentia mea tantum, sed multo magis nunc in absentia mea, *cum metu et tremore vestram salutem operamini.* Deus est enim qui operatur in vobis et velle, et perficere pro bona voluntate" (Philipp. ii. 12, 13).

[13] Bergier, *Traité de la Relig.* vol. x. § 6, pp. 255, seq. Paris Edit. 1780.

[14] Bergier, as above, and *Tableau de la Miser. div.* pp. 265, seq.

[15] Tur. Edit. 1771.

their controversy with the irreligious, concur in this interpretation of the text.

The Council of Trent itself confirms it[16] by superadding the text from the First Epistle to the Corinthians [17] "He that thinketh himself to stand, let him take heed lest he fall," to the one above cited, "with fear and trembling work out your salvation;" meaning thereby that in all humility and mistrust of ourselves we ought to recur to the necessary means to avert our fall, being perfectly assured that when we on our side have done what little we can, God in His great mercy will help us to persevere.

Cornelius à Lapide[18] also explains this fear to mean that humility and distrust in ourselves with which we should work, in order that the Lord may continue His graces to us. He remarks that this twelfth verse is joined to the antecedent ones by means of the adverb "Wherefore," as if the Apostle meant to say to the Philippians: "I have exhorted you[19] to fly all discord and contention by the practice of humility, obedience, and conformity with the example of Jesus Christ, Who humbled Himself and obeyed even unto the death of the Cross;[20] even so I exhort you also to humble yourselves, in order that you may be exalted with Him; and to be obedient, and work out your salvation, not with pride and contention, but with humility and trembling."

The same commentator next cites the authority of St. Augustine, who says that "as God works in us, we ought on our side to humble ourselves, in order that we may the more readily receive His graces. Nor ought we to wonder that God resists the proud, and gives His grace to the humble; for grace is like rain, which over-

---

[16] Sess. vi. chap. 13.   [17] 1 Cor. x. 12.   [18] Vol. xiii. p. 454.
[19] Philipp. ii. 2, 3.   [20] *Ibid*. ii. 8.

flows the valley, whilst the summits of the mountains it leaves parched."[21]

St. Anselm says substantially the same thing.[22]

Father Segneri also says that "fear and trembling mean the keeping ourselves humble, because we have need of God's grace in order to work; and the result He most desires from our fear and trembling is that we should always keep close to Him . . . and the consequence of this is that we invoke and supplicate Him, and so in the end come to be saved in the midst of the storm."[23]

This interpretation is also in accordance with the meaning of the First Epistle to the Corinthians ii. 3, in which fear and trembling must be understood in the sense of distrust in oneself, not distrust in God's help.

St. John Chrysostom, explaining the meaning of "with fear and trembling,"[24] says: "Work not carelessly, but

[21] "It is God Who works in us, therefore with fear and trembling make yourselves a valley to catch the rain; the low lands are overflowed, the high grounds are parched, grace is the rainfall: why then wonder that God resists the proud, and gives grace to the humble? Wherefore with fear and trembling, that is, with *humility:* let not thy aims be high, but fear: fear, that thou mayest be filled: aim not high, lest thou be parched" (*De verb. Apost.* lib. ii.).

[22] "Therefore with fear and trembling, lest in consequence of attributing good works to themselves they should be extolled for them as if they were their own, . . . lest mayhap that which is given to the humble be taken away from the proud" (St. Anselm, on the same). "For it is God Who worketh in you, both to will and to accomplish."

[23] Father Segneri's *Manna dell' anima*, May 2.

[24] "With fear and trembling, . . . that is to say, do your work, not carelessly, but with attention to all details, and extraordinary zeal. Let not what I have said to you about fear and trembling inspire you with fear; for I have not spoken thus in order to cause you to despair, but to induce you to apply your mental faculties, and to prevent your becoming languid and yielding to weariness. If you follow this injunction, trust me God will work out everything, for it is God Who worketh in you" (Serm. viii. *On Epist. to the Philipp.* vol. iv. p. 1031).

with the utmost diligence and attention." But this attention itself he tempers by the confidence which the words of the Apostle in the thirteenth verse, immediately following, are calculated to inspire. "Be not affrighted by what I said of fear and trembling," adds the holy Doctor, "since my object in saying it was not to banish hope, but to induce thee to exercise diligence, and not to slacken, and almost invite failure. Do thou but supply this diligence, and God will do all the rest; in Him put thy trust, for it is God Who works in us."

Observe, moreover, that the text in question is found in the same Epistle wherein St. Paul exhorts the Philippians to spiritual joy, saying, "Rejoice in the Lord always; again, I say, rejoice." [25] Now how could fear and trembling for the issue of their eternal salvation co-exist with the rejoicing which he inculcates at the same time with so much earnestness? In fact he immediately adds: "Be nothing solicitous: but in everything by prayer and supplication with thanksgiving let your petitions be made known to God. And the peace of God, which surpasseth all understanding, keep your hearts and minds in Christ Jesus."[26]

In a word, the Apostle desires, says Mgr. Martini, "that we should work out our salvation with fear and trembling, that is to say, with a holy and humble solicitude of spirit, in order that being always fearful of ourselves, and distrustful of our own strength, we may the more confide in God." In other words, he exhorts us to a holy, filial fear; which, at the same time that it warns us to use every precaution against displeasing God by sin, will also induce us to rest our assured confidence in Him. For the Apostle styles Him the God, not of fear, but of hope, and has for his object that God may fill us, not with fear, but with all joy and peace in

[25] Philipp. iv. 4.   [26] Philipp. iv. 6, 7.

believing, and that we may abound in hope, casting all our care on Him, for He will have care of us.[27]

Next as to the other text which says: "Serve ye the Lord with fear,"[28] it is to be observed that the words are here especially addressed to kings and to those who exercise judgment on earth;[29] and even with respect to them St. Jerome remarks that, although God wishes to excite their fears lest their elevation to supreme power should engender pride, He nevertheless fails not to administer comfort immediately afterwards, by bidding them rejoice in the midst of that fear which He enjoins.[30]

Moreover, Menochius in his commentaries, and St. Liguori in his translation of the Psalms, both say that according to the Hebrew text this word fear should be rendered godliness, or the filial fear wherewith kings and judges are bound to serve God. For this reason the Saint translates these two verses thus: "You, then, O kings, who judge the earth, learn to understand your duty, and to perform it well. Serve the Lord with filial fear, and with gladness."

If, then, God desired that the Hebrews, who were under a law of fear, should regard Him as a God of goodness, and fear Him it is true, but with filial and reverential fear, not excluding true spiritual gladness—as He proved by the many times He called upon all to serve Him with a holy joy[31]—how much more does

---

[27] "Now the God of *hope* fill you with all joy and peace in believing: that you may abound in *hope*" (Rom. xv. 13). "Casting all your care upon Him, for He hath care of you" (1 St. Peter v. 7).

[28] Psalm ii. 11.

[29] "And now, O ye kings, understand: receive instruction, you that judge the earth" (Psalm ii. 10).

[30] "And rejoice unto him with trembling" (Psalm ii. 11).

[31] "Think of the Lord in goodness" (Wisdom i. 1). "Be glad in the Lord, and rejoice, ye just" (Psalm xxxi. 11). "Sing joyfully to God, all the earth: serve ye the Lord with gladness" (Psalm xcix. 1, and elsewhere).

the Lord desire to be feared by us with a fear that is filial, to whom, as the Apostle says, He hath not given a spirit of fear, but of power and of love;[32] by us who, according to St. Anselm, have not received, like the Jews, the spirit of servitude, that prompts to servile fear, but the spirit of love and grace becoming children of adoption, by virtue of which we with the utmost tenderness and affection call God by the sweet name of Father.[33]

CHAPTER II.

Whether moral certainty of being in a state of grace and of the pardon of sin is attainable in the Christian religion.

FIRST DIFFICULTY.—A Divine religion should fill the heart with peace, whereas the Christian religion drives peace away, by pronouncing an eternity of woe against those who die at enmity with God, at the same time that it makes its followers live in continual uncertainty as to the state of their conscience, by reason of its teaching the lesson that we never know "whether we be worthy of love or hatred,"[1] no matter how faithfully we endeavour to fulfil God's law. As death, then, may overtake us at any moment, it is impossible for us, little as we are capable of realizing that eternity of woe, to

---

[32] "For God hath not given us the spirit of *fear*: but of power and of love" (2 Tim. i. 7).

[33] "For you have not received the spirit of bondage again in fear: but you have received the spirit of adoption of sons, whereby we cry: Abba, Father" (Rom. viii. 15). See also Cornelius à Lapide on this subject.

[1] "Man knoweth not whether he be worthy of love or hatred" (Eccles. ix. 1).

Solution of Difficulties.

live exempt from the gravest apprehension of dying in sin and being eternally damned.

Answer.—Bergier,[2] in replying on the question of uncertainty here alluded to, rests his answer upon Ecclesiastes itself, and states that here uncertainty has reference to the object with which the Lord visits us with afflictions, as we know not whether they be intended for our punishment or purification. Just as in like manner when He sends us prosperity we know not whether it be meant for our reward or as an invitation to good. In short, says Ecclesiastes, we know not if we are worthy of love or hatred; all must remain uncertain until the advent of futurity. And why? The reason is, because, so far as temporal events are in question, they all befall alike the just and the wicked.[3]

But even if this text be understood in a sense opposite to the foregoing, we must not conclude from it that the Lord has given us up to such a state of uncertainty as would rob us of peace of mind, and consign us to a life of constant fear and apprehension. For although when Holy Church, the true interpreter of Holy Writ, at the Council of Trent condemned the heresy of those who, rejecting the Sacrament of Penance, held that for justification it was only necessary to believe as of Divine faith that they were justified, she explained and defined that we cannot know with the certainty of Divine faith whether we be in favour or disfavour with God,[4] yet she at the same time condemned not, nor did she prohibit that moral certainty which suffices to re-assure

---

[2] Bergier, l.c. tom. xii. pp. 126, § 19; Edit. Paris, 1784, p. 133.

[3] "All things are kept uncertain for the time to come, because all things happen equally to the just and the wicked, to the good and to the evil. . . . As the good, so also is the sinner" (Eccles. ix. 2).

[4] "For no one can possibly know with the infallible certainty of faith that he has obtained favour with God" (Sess. vi. cap. 9, *De Justif.*).

us and remove every rational doubt of our being or not being in a state of grace.

Nay, not only does the Church not condemn or prohibit this moral certainty, she has been ever foremost to recognize it. Thus she sets before us in the Divine office the lesson taken from the Thirteenth Homily of St. Gregory, Pope, on St. Luke's Gospel, "Let your loins be girt," wherein he lays down that whosoever is assured of hope in God, united with the testimony of his own conscience to the goodness of his actions, willingly dies, and presents himself joyfully before his Judge in order to reap his reward.[5]

Add to this that the moral certainty here spoken of is so essential a condition of mind, that in its absence no one should dare to approach the Table of the Lord, for, as the Apostle Paul teaches,[6] in order to approach it worthily, it is necessary to have a well-grounded confidence in the grace of God.

SECOND DIFFICULTY.—But now I hear some persons object, how often, precisely on account of this uncertainty, do we abstain from Holy Communion? For who is there that can be assured of never having committed a mortal sin, or of having been pardoned after committing one?

Answer.—In the first place we reply that the practice, both of the Church and of the directors of consciences, as well as of the faithful, generally presupposes the existence of this moral certainty. How, in point of fact, could the Church impose on the faithful the obli-

---

[5] "He that is *assured* in his hope and his work, opens the door at once when he hears a knock, because he *joyfully* faces his judge and *exults* at the prospect of a glorious recompense" (Lect. ix. *De Comm. Conf. non Pont.*).

[6] "But let a man prove himself, and so let him eat of that bread" (1 Cor. xi. 28).

gation of communicating at Easter, if the assured confidence of freedom from sin and of being consequently in a state of grace, were unattainable? If such were the case, how could directors of consciences take upon themselves to counsel, and when they have to deal with the timid or scrupulous, to command the penitent to approach the Holy Communion? In fine, how could the faithful themselves obey such an injunction if, after having, with God's assistance, complied with all the requirements of duty, they still failed to be morally certain of being in a state of grace.

When the Church therefore prohibits him who is conscious of being in a state of mortal sin from approaching the Table of the Lord,[7] and simultaneously commands us all to approach it at Easter, she must infer the existence of this moral certainty in each one's conscience, agreeably to the saying of St. John, that if conscience do not reproach us with grievous sin, we may rest at ease and trust in God that we are in His grace.[8]

Mgr. Martini also in this sense explains the text from St. John. "If," he says, "conscience do not reproach us, let us have confidence before God." Father Segneri, too, in his explanation of the verse in the *Miserere*, "To my hearing thou shalt give joy and gladness," refers the joy here spoken of to the well-grounded opinion of our being in a state of grace, resulting from the absence of the reproaches of conscience, and supports his assertion by the authority of the text from St. John just quoted.

In the next place, if we take the case of our conscience

[7] "Let a man prove himself." The practice of the Church enjoins the necessity of this probation, so that no one conscious to himself of mortal sin ought to approach the Holy Eucharist without first having recourse to sacramental confession" (Sess. xiii. cap. 7, *De Euch.* and caps. 9, 11).

[8] "Dearly beloved, if our heart do not reprehend us, we have confidence towards God" (1 St. John iii. 21).

reproaching us with the commission of mortal sin, we have either duly confessed it, or we have not. If we have duly confessed it and received absolution, we are morally certain of having received pardon in virtue of the power given by Jesus Christ to His ministers when He said: "Whose sins you shall forgive, they are forgiven them."[9] And if we have not as yet duly confessed it, have we not in confession a prompt and efficacious means of reconciliation with God? Let us have recourse to the Lord; let us by His aid excite in ourselves the true sorrow of perfect contrition; let us resolve to confess without delay, and we may be morally certain of pardon, even before confession. Such is, without exception, the teaching of the Church contained in her Catechisms and drawn from the decision of the Council of Trent, namely, that perfect contrition at once, and even before he has approached the Sacrament of Penance,[10] justifies the sinner.

THIRD DIFFICULTY.—Who can assure us that we have made a good confession, and that, instead of obtaining pardon, we have not been guilty of an awful sacrilege?

Answer.—We can be as sure of having made a good confession as we can be of having sinned. What is it, in fact, that accuses and convicts us of sin? Unquestionably our own conscience, which warns us that we have advisedly and of malice prepense transgressed some commandment of God or of the Church in an important particular. Now this identical conscience can in like

[9] St. John xx. 23.
[10] "The moment we conceive this contrition in the mind, the remission of our sins is vouchsafed by God, as is declared by those words of the Prophet: 'I said I will confess against myself my injustice to the Lord, and thou hast forgiven the wickedness of my sin' (Psalm xxxi. 5)" (*Catech. Rom.* p. 2, cap. de Pœnit. n. 34).

manner testify that we have worthily confessed. In proof that this is so, St. Paul says [11] that "his conscience bears testimony" that he always demeaned himself in a special manner towards the Corinthians, with all simplicity and sincerity of heart before God; and further bids the Hebrews,[12] as Mgr. Martini, supported by St. John Chrysostom, explains his words, pray for him, as he deemed himself not unworthy of their prayers, seeing that "his good conscience assured him" that he was not, as some would have them believe, an apostate from the law, or a hypocrite, but a preacher who had preached the word of God with sincerity. It is this same testimony of conscience alone that St. Paul, as we observed before, exhorts the faithful to sift before approaching Holy Communion. The probation which the Apostle enjoins is nothing more than an inquiry conducted with sincerity into the question whether our conscience reproach us with any grievous sin committed and not duly confessed.[13]

Adverting next to the opinions of the holy Fathers on this question, St. Basil says that "if we experience in our own interior a hatred of sin, we may be assured that it has been pardoned to us."[14] St. Augustine says: "Think of me (O Secondinus) as thou pleasest, for it matters not to me what thy thoughts are, provided my own conscience accuse me not before God." And he

[11] "For our glory is this, *the testimony of our conscience*, that in simplicity of heart and sincerity of God, and not in carnal wisdom, we have conversed in this world" (2 Cor. i. 12).

[12] "Pray for us. *For we trust we have a good conscience*" (Heb. xiii. 18. *Vide* Cornelius à Lapide).

[13] *Vide* Suarez, vol. viii. L ix. cap. ii. n. 3, seq.

[14] "How can a man be *firmly assured* that God has remitted his sins? Undoubtedly he may, if he be of the same temper of mind with him who exclaimed: 'I hated my iniquity,' &c. . . . In such case he may *believe without hesitation* that he is free from sin" (*In Reg. Brev. disp. interrog.* 296).

says in another passage "that the testimony of conscience affords us a certain means of knowing if our faith be sincere, our hope strong, and our charity unfeigned."[15] St. Isidore says that "the conscience is clean when it neither can justly accuse us of past sins, nor wickedly feels complacency in the present commission of them."[16] Observe that he uses the expression "justly accuse" to signify that we are to disregard all scruples; and that remorse, in order to convince us of mortal sin, must rest on solid foundations.

And although the Council of Trent lays it down that, as no one of the faithful ought to doubt the mercy of God, the merits of Jesus Christ, or the efficacy and value of the sacraments, so may every one, having regard only to his own inherent weakness, entertain fears of his not being in the grace of God, not having the assurance thereof by Divine faith. Nevertheless be it observed that the words of the Council are, that *we ought* not to doubt the mercy of God, and that *we may* fear as regards grace, for the reason alleged, namely, because we have no assurance by Divine faith.[17]

Hence the celebrated Suarez goes the length of saying that we may have that certainty which strictly and morally excludes actual fear, and adds that a just man

---

[15] "Think what thou pleasest about Augustine, *provided only* that my *conscience* do not accuse me before God" (*Cont. Secund.* cap. i. tom. vi.). "It is as it were the boast of conscience, that it informs you whether your faith is whole, your hope certain, and your charity unfeigned" (*In Psalm* cxlix.).

[16] "That conscience is clean which neither justly accuses one of past sins, nor unjustly delights in present ones" (St. Isidore).

[17] "In the same manner as no religiously minded person ought to doubt of the mercy of God, the merits of Christ, or the virtue and efficacy of the sacraments, so may every one, having regard to his own innate weakness, fear and tremble with respect to his being in a state of grace, since no one can know with the infallible assurance of faith that he has attained to the grace of God" (Sess. vi. cap. 9).

can even attain to the same certainty that his actual sins have been remitted in confession as he has that his original sin was remitted in baptism.[18]

Although doubts as to our having knowingly harboured or consented to sin in thought may sometimes torment us, it does not thence follow that we can be in any uncertainty as to the dispositions requisite for making a good confession. Conscience can have no rational doubt on this head, if we are conscious of having fulfilled the necessary conditions, and fulfilled them with deliberation, solicitude, and an earnest desire to succeed, laying ourselves out for the work, and going over it again and again whenever we suspect that we have been wanting in fervour, after having, by a preliminary prayer, invoked the assistance of God's grace towards its due accomplishment. There can be no doubt but that the conditions necessary for a good confession, when fulfilled in this spirit, are carefully and deliberately performed. If, on the other hand, we approach the Sacrament only through human respect, or without renouncing dangerous occasions and evil habits, or without resolving, when able, to make restitution, or without pardoning our enemies, or in such like bad dispositions, conscience, which cannot be unaware of or ignore this deliberate result, will, in a manner not to be mistaken, charge us with sacrilege. Conscience too, if we hearken to her voice, warns us of any grave deliberate negligence with respect to our examination or

---

[18] "Nevertheless this should be added, that we may attain to such a degree of certainty as, according to the ordinary course of things and morally speaking, should exclude any actual alarm" (Tract. viii. *De Grat.* l. ix. cap. xi. n. 10). "Wherefore I deem it in the highest degree probable that it is possible for a just man to reach a state of virtue wherein he shall be no less assured of the remission of the sins he may have actually committed than he is of the remission of his original sin" (*Ibid.* nn. 12, 13).

sorrow for sin, whereby our confession may have been rendered sacrilegious; or of any want of sorrow, the result of insufficient reflection, whereby it may have been rendered null.

FOURTH DIFFICULTY.—If conscience could assure us of being in the grace of God, how came St. Paul to say "that although his conscience did not reproach him with sin, he did not on that account deem himself justified?"[19]

Answer.—St. Paul does not here deny his justification, but only refuses to rest it on the mere silence of conscience, our justification being not the result of the testimony of conscience, but the effect of grace. Therefore he says not simply "yet am I not justified," but "I am not justified hereby," thus no more excluding from his calculation moral certainty than does Ecclesiastes by the text before cited, which merely negatives the existence of the certainty derived from Divine faith, "since no one can know with the certainty of faith which is infallible," as we pointed out before, and as Suarez, surnamed the Eminent Doctor by Benedict XIV., has abundantly proved.[20]

Herewith also agrees Mgr. Martini, who in his commentary on the words of the Apostle, in his note on verses 3 and 4, writes: "for although conscience lays nothing to my charge, it does not *on that account* follow that I possess an infallible certainty of justification."

Lastly, the text from St. Paul, if understood in the sense we impugn, would be a contradiction of that passage in St. John wherein he bids us have confidence in God that we have obtained pardon.[21]

---

[19] "I am not conscious to myself of anything, yet am I not hereby justified" (1 Cor. iv. 4).
[20] Tom. viii. l. ix. cap. iv. seq.
[21] 1 St. John iii. 21.

Solution of Difficulties.

FIFTH DIFFICULTY.—It is laid down in numerous ascetical works that "the just man falls seven times a day."[22] Holy King David—according to St. Augustine's translation of his words as given in the commentaries of Mgr. Martini—in his terror exclaims, "Who can understand sins? Cleanse me, O Lord! from such of mine as are hidden from me, and pardon me such as I have been the occasion of in others."[23] Now if the just man falls so often, and if so holy a King and Prophet felt such fears respecting his hidden sins, how much more reason have we, who transgress so frequently, and are therefore much more likely to have some mortal sin hidden from us, or some sin of scandal either unknown to or not sufficiently repaired by us—to dread the displeasure of God?

Answer.—We reply in the first place with Cornelius à Lapide, that although Cassian[24] and certain codices affirm, as objected above, "that the just man falls seven times a day;" yet the words "a day" do not occur in the Hebrew or the Septuagint, any more than in the Vulgate, which we are bound to follow—the genuine text running thus: "A just man shall fall seven times, and shall rise again; but the wicked shall fall down into evil."[25]

In the second place, as some interpret these words, the fall of the just man here spoken of has reference to his fall into many tribulations from which the Lord will deliver him,[26] according to the language used in the 33rd Psalm; while others explain them as meaning

---

[22] "The just man shall fall seven times a day" (*Vide* Du Clot. v. iv. p. 372, *La Bible vengée*).

[23] "Who can understand sins? From my secret ones cleanse me, O Lord, and from those of others spare thy servant" (Psalm xviii. 13, 14).

[24] Col. 22, chap. xiv.

[25] Prov. xxiv. 16.

[26] "Many are the afflictions of the just: but out of them all will the Lord deliver them" (Psalm xxxiii. 20).

SIXTH DIFFICULTY.—How can a man who has had the misfortune to fall into mortal sin ever attain to certainty of his reinstatement in God's grace, seeing that even after he has made use of all the means suggested and prescribed by the Christian religion, and done all in his power to obtain pardon for his sin, this same religion teaches that, all his efforts notwithstanding, *no one can ever be certain of having succeeded;* that, in fact, the Wise Man warns us "not to be without fear about sin forgiven."[30] Say, is it possible to find peace in such a religion, and how then can it be Divine?

Answer.—It is right to premise that in some manuscripts the phrase used is, "Be not without fear about the forgiveness of sin." Nevertheless, according to the Vulgate, the words used are, "Be not without fear about sin forgiven." Some commentators understand by this text that our fear should regard the uncertainty of pardon for past sins; others understand it of the uncertainty of pardon for sin committed in the future.

With regard to the first meaning, it is true that we cannot have certainty of Divine faith that our past sins have been forgiven, in the absence of a Divine revelation that we have fulfilled all the conditions required for obtaining pardon. We can, however, as was before observed, attain to a moral certainty of having done so, when our conscience does not accuse us of having omitted any of the conditions necessary for a good confession, or when we are conscious of having had perfect contrition accompanied by a desire to confess.

We may therefore here fittingly remark, that to refer the fear in question to the uncertainty of the pardon of past sins involves a contradiction; for when we are told, "Be not without fear about sin forgiven," the pardon of the sin is implied, and to attach such a

[30] "De propitiato peccato noli esse sine metu" (Ecclus. v. 5).

perfect consciousness, for as philosophers hold "nothing is voluntary unless it be premeditated," and all theologians admit that in order to make a sin mortal it must be not only grave as to matter, but voluntary as to the manner of commission, and therefore the object of perfect consciousness. It is not, I repeat, very easy to commit sins such as I have described, and then forget them, for, as David[29] confesses to have happened in his case, the sin is always before you and is ever gnawing at your conscience.

As to the case of those who, after a dissolute course of life, return to the Lord, and, notwithstanding a diligent examination of conscience, omit some sins in confession through forgetfulness, it is beyond doubt that all their sins, without exception of the forgotten and hidden ones, are wiped away by forgiveness, although the obligation to confess them later, whenever remembered or brought to light, still remains.

Lastly, as to the scandals we have occasioned, we may be assured of forgiveness when we have made, or sincerely resolved to make, full and as far as possible complete reparation in the manner prescribed by our confessor, and by furnishing in our own person an example of a Christian life. And we have nothing more to add, but our earnest prayer to God that He would Himself supply any deficiency in our reparation, by enlightening and converting those to whom we have been the occasion of sin. All theologians concur in this teaching. We may add in conclusion that, according to Mgr. Martini, the text in question signifies in the Hebrew, "Keep me far off from the proud," and in the Vulgate might be interpreted, "Keep me far off from unbelievers or strangers, or aliens in religion."

[29] "My sin is always before me" (Psalm l. 5).

although God out of His great goodness has not punished thy past sins, yet for this very reason fear and beware how thou abusest that goodness by sinning in the future; deceive not thyself by reliance on the greatness of His mercy, saying, "Great is the goodness of the Lord: He will have mercy on the multitude of my sins;" for though He have readily pardoned your past sins, it may nevertheless come to pass, if you add sin unto sin, that His chastisements, justly provoked by the abuse of His mercy, shall suddenly overtake you.[33]

It follows from the foregoing that whosoever bewails, or is resolved to bewail, detest, and abandon his sins, has every ground for hoping that he has obtained or is about to obtain pardon for them; but that whosoever is obstinately bent on abusing the mercy of God by offending Him in time to come in consequence of the confidence inspired by His mercy in the past, has every reason to fear the heaviest punishment. He should reflect that although God has promised pardon to the sinner who sues for it in a penitential spirit, He has never promised the sinner time for repentance. Death may surprise him in his sin, and make him a victim to his rash confidence.

SEVENTH DIFFICULTY.—But if religion, while it bids its followers to hope, and to neglect no means necessary for conversion, as long as life remains, tells us at the same time that it is in vain for any one, who has overstepped the limit of sin prescribed for him, to try, no matter what his efforts, to return to God, who can be assured that he has not overstepped the prescribed limit? Is not the very foundation of the assured hope that is enjoined on us under pain of eternal damnation, utterly removed? Can a religion, then, whose doctrines are

[33] Cornelius à Lapide, p. 112.

thus contradictory and desolating, be Divine? And yet such was the message conveyed to the inhabitants of Damascus, who were told *that up to the third, but yet not up to the fourth sin, might they have been pardoned.* [34]

Answer.—The Catholic Church has never taught that God so far abandons the sinner during his lifetime as to withhold from him the aids necessary for his conversion, or be unwilling to pardon him. "Assuredly," says St. Augustine,[35] "God makes not void His oft-repeated promises not only of pardon to the sinner, but of the complete cancelling and utter oblivion of his iniquities, provided he sues for pardon with a contrite heart."[36] Nor would it be consistent with God's own nature to indulge in mockery towards His creatures, as He would be doing if He enjoined on them impossibilities; and if, while He protested that He desired not the death of the sinner, but rather that he might be converted and live,[37] He abandoned him to his own unaided efforts, utterly incapable, as He knew them to be, of any progress towards eternal life.[38]

Now, as it would be a gross calumny against the Church to accuse her of propounding, in her teachings, an idea of God so utterly false and insulting, let us examine how the above countervailing text is explained by the sacred commentators and the holy Fathers.

---

[34] "For three crimes of Damascus and for four I will not convert it" (Amos i. 3).

[35] "So completely gracious is God, that in His judgments there is no revenge, no hurry in His condemnations, nor even in imputing guilt does His love wax cold" (*De dilig. Deo,* cap. xii.).

[36] "If the wicked do penance ... I will not remember all his iniquities" (Ezech. xviii. 21, 22).

[37] "I desire not the death of the wicked, but that the wicked turn from his way and live" (Ezech. xxxiii. 11).

[38] "Without Me you can do nothing" (St. John xv. 5).

Tirinus interprets and paraphrases this text thus: "By reason of the multitude of its iniquities, but more especially of the fourth sin, which exceeded all the rest in enormity, I will no more pardon them, that is to say, I will not again recall the decree issued by Me against them of chastisement, punishment, destruction, and death."[39] In support of this interpretation he cites the Chaldean paraphrast, St. Jerome, Albertus Magnus, Hugo, Pagninus, Sanchez, and Cornelius à Lapide, who all concur in offering the same interpretation, as does also Mgr. Martini.

The Antiochean Arabic version, quoted by Cornelius à Lapide, gives the following as the words of the text: "I will not lead them back any more into their own land;"[40] and Sanchez, who is referred to by Cornelius à Lapide, gives the words as: "I will not deliver them from that death of which I have pronounced sentence against them."[41] In a word, almost all concur in explaining this text to be a solemn declaration by God of His intention not to revoke His sentence of temporal punishment which had gone forth against the inhabitants of Damascus for their past iniquities, but chiefly for their enormous iniquity in inflicting upon the Israelites a death of exquisite cruelty. In this sense Theodoret, cited by the above-named Cornelius à Lapide,

---

[39] "'On account of three,' meaning thereby several, 'crimes of Damascus, but especially in consequence of the fourth,' as the Syriac and Arabic versions have it, 'I will not convert her.' In other words, I will not remit the sentence of punishment, chastisement, destruction, or death passed by Me upon the people of Damascus" (Tirin. on this passage).

[40] "I will not convert that people," that is, I will not recall them from captivity into their own land.

[41] "I will not convert them," in other words, I will not recall them from death, . . . that is to say, I will not recall them from this particular death.

Menochius, and Mgr. Martini, all understand this text.[42]

St. Jerome, also cited by Cornelius à Lapide, paraphrases the text as follows: "I have waited long for the people of Damascus in the hope that they would repent, and when they offended I abstained from punishment, that they might be at last converted and received into grace; but since, instead of being converted, they return a third and a fourth time to the same iniquities, I must change My hand and administer correction by tribulation and afflictions."[43]

"God," says St. Gregory, "is patient and long-suffering; but when He finds that the sinner, instead of profiting by the time and graces accorded to him, merely abuses them and becomes more obstinate in sin, He removes him from the world by a sudden and unprovided death."[44] St. Augustine also states it as his opinion, that "when the sinner has filled up the measure of his iniquity, God visits him with death. It is a rational belief," he says, "that the Divine patience bears with every sinner until he has filled up the predestined number of sins, and that as soon as this number is completed God at once inflicts on him the punishment of death,[45] whereupon

---

[42] By three and by four he means a multitude, that is to say, a countless number of iniquities.

[43] "I have waited long to see if Damascus would repent of her wickedness, and I willed not to punish her sins, in the hope that she might be restored to health, but inasmuch as she repeated the same crimes for the third and fourth time, I am compelled to alter My purpose, and to deal punishment on her delinquencies."

[44] "He is suddenly carried off who has been borne with long."

[45] "It is reasonable to believe, that the patience of God endures every one until he has completed the measure of his sins and reached their limit, and that after this consummation he is at once struck down without a hope of pardon" (Lib. *De Vit. Christ.* cap. iii.).

the soul[46] goes forth and the door of pardon is for ever closed."

St. Liguori, in his sermon[47] for the First Sunday of Lent, on the multitude of sins, after adducing the instance of Baltassar, ends by exclaiming: "Oh! how many meet with the same fate! After a long career of offences against God, when the number of their sins has reached a certain point, they are surprised by death and buried in Hell!"

And although the punishment of a sudden and unprovided death is most terrible, it would be, according to St. Ambrose, a far more terrible punishment for the sinner to be allowed to live on; for it is far more detrimental to him to live on, and obstinately adhere to sin, than to die in sin; for the obstinate sinner, so long as life lasts, is ever adding to his sin, and consequently to the severity of his punishment through all eternity.[48] St. Bernard also says that it is better for the sinner, whose soul, through sin, leads in life a living death, that his body should quickly die.[49]

This opinion agrees also with that of Rupert, who asserts the fourth unforgiven sin of the people of Damascus to have been final impenitence. Indeed, it must be evident that so long as the sinner fails to detest and abandon his sin, God cannot pardon him.

In conclusion, it is laid down by St. John Chrysostom,

[46] See the testimony of St. John Chrysostom at the end of this difficulty.

[47] Serm. xv.

[48] "Death is bitter to the wicked man, and yet life is still more bitter than death to him, for it is more calamitous to live to sin than to die in sin. For the wicked man, the longer he lives, the more he augments his sin; dying, he shall cease to sin" (Lib. *De bono mortis*, cap. ii.).

[49] "It is expedient for him who is dead as to his soul, to die also as to his body" (Serm. *De fallac. præs. vitæ*).

that God in His mercy is ever ready to pardon the sinner who from his heart and with genuine contrition repents of his sins—a truth we shall find developed in the following pages.[50]

CHAPTER III.

The meaning to be attached to the phrase "the hardness and blindness of sinners."

FIRST DIFFICULTY.—How can it be said that the Lord God desires that the sinner should be converted and live, if at the very time that He imposes on him the obligation of being converted and of believing and hoping in Him, He hardens his heart and blinds his eyes so as to render his conversion impossible? Herein does not God show Himself a cruel and unjust tyrant? Does He not hereby become the author of their sins, and of their very damnation? And yet that He acts in this manner is quite plain from the passage in Holy Writ where He is described as saying to Moses—"I have hardened the heart of Pharao and the heart of his servants, that I may work these My signs in him."[1]

Answer.—In the first place it is to be observed that there are two equivocal forms of expression of very ordinary occurrence in every language. One occurs when we say

---

[50] "Hast sinned? Repent. Hast sinned again? Repent again. Hast sinned a thousand times? Repent a thousand times. Whilst breath is in thy body, nay, whilst, so to speak, thou art breathing out thy soul on the bed of death, and art passing over the threshold of this world, the mercy of God outstrips the swiftness of time" (Hom. ii. *in Psalm.* l.).

[1] Exodus x. 1; Bergier, l.c. tom. vi. p. 30, cap. clxxxv.; tom. ix. p. 83.

of a person that he does a thing which he has not prevented, though he had the power to do so. Of this we have an instance in that passage of Exodus where Moses, seeing the increasing hardships heaped upon the children of Israel by Pharao in consequence of his request that they should be allowed to depart, addressed himself to the Lord and said, "Lord, why hast Thou afflicted this people?"[2] Here Moses attributes the afflictions of the people to their non-prevention by God. The other occurs where that which is only the occasion is spoken of as the cause of an event; as for instance when a father is said to spoil his son by excessive fondness, or when we say to an acquaintance, "You made me very angry," meaning only that he was the occasion of our anger.

Moreover it is right also to remark that the Hebrew particle, which is always translated by the Latin equivalent *ut* Anglicé *that*, should often be rendered into Latin by the words *ita ut* Anglicé *so that*. An example of such a rendering of the particle occurs in Exodus,[3] where the text runs—"Pharao will not hear you *that* many signs may be done in the land of Egypt"—*Non audiet vos Pharao, ut multa signa fiant in terra Egypti*. When Pharao refused to listen to Moses, his object in doing so certainly was not in order to bring down manifold scourges on himself and his people. Therefore the accurate rendering of the Hebrew text is as follows—"Pharao will not hear you, by reason whereof I will do great signs."

Lastly, remember, that it is of faith that God wills not, but rather detests, sin. It is solemnly affirmed in Ecclesiasticus that He has never commanded any man to do

---

[2] "Lord, why hast Thou afflicted this people? . . . For since he time I went in to Pharao, . . . he hath afflicted this people, and Thou hast not delivered them" (Exodus v. 22, 23).

[3] Exodus xi. 9.

Solution of Difficulties.

evil; nor ever, as Cornelius à Lapide explains the Greek text, given a license for its commission, or when committed allowed it to pass unpunished, and desireth not to increase the number of unfaithful and unprofitable children.[4] Nay, more, it is utterly impossible, in consequence of His infinite holiness and perfection, that God could ever will the existence of sin.

Hence, although God might suffer the heart of Pharao to become hardened and obstinate, in consequence of his malice, or in other words might not prevent this from happening, as in the case mentioned in the Book of Wisdom, it was quite impossible that He could ever have hardened him in evil.

So much being premised, we may now turn to the above-cited text from Exodus, and render it as follows— "I will permit Pharao in the blindness of his own malice to become hardened," in other words, "I will not prevent him from becoming hardened, in order that I may use the conquering of his obstinacy as an occasion for performing mighty works and wonders."[5]

And Moses frequently repeats that Pharao was verily hardened of his own free will; as, for instance, when he records that Pharao would not yield, and that he hardened his heart, and turned a deaf ear to Moses and Aaron, and to the commands of God, as soon as he was delivered from the plague of frogs; and further on, that he added to his sin, and that the hearts of himself and his servants were hardened exceedingly, nor would he suffer the people to depart, as the Lord had com-

---

[4] "Because thou art not a God that willest iniquity" (Psalm v. 5). "Thou hast loved justice and hatedst iniquity" (Psalm xliv. 8). "He hath commanded no man to do wickedly, and He hath given no man license to sin" (Ecclus. xv. 21). "For He desireth not a multitude of faithless and unprofitable children" (Ecclus. xv. 22).

[5] Exodus x. 1, 2.

manded, when there came a respite from the storms of rain, hail, and lightning.[6]

It is to be observed that in the Hebrew text instead of the words, "his heart was hardened," the expression used is, "he hardened his own heart," so that, as Cornelius à Lapide remarks, wherever the Vulgate has "his heart was hardened," we should understand that Pharao hardened his heart, or rather his will; for blindness is a property of the understanding, and hardness of the will.

Moreover, there would be a manifest contradiction in God's sending Moses ten times to Pharao, with a demand for permission for the Hebrew people to depart and offer sacrifices to Him in the wilderness, and in His, at the same time, hardening Pharao's heart in order to their retention in bondage; this in effect would be at one and the same time to will that they should depart, by His frequent commands to them to that effect, and not to will it, by His action on the heart of Pharao in order to prevent their departure.

Nay, if Pharao had hardened his heart in obedience to the Divine will, he would not, as Cornelius à Lapide well remarks, have sinned, for the will of God is the proper standard to which every will that merits the name of good should conform.

Let us in addition reflect on the number of plagues

---

[6] "And *he turned himself away*, and went into his house, neither *did he set his heart* to it this time also" (Exodus vii. 23). "And Pharao seeing that rest was given, hardened his own heart" (viii. 15). "And Pharao seeing that the rain and the hail and the thunders were ceased, increased his sin, and his heart was hardened, and the heart of his servants, and it was made exceeding hard, neither did he let the children of Israel go, as the Lord had commanded by the hand of Moses" (ix. 34, 35).

wherewith Pharao was afflicted because he would not suffer the people to depart.[7]

Now, as St. Fulgentius[8] remarks, it is impossible that God would punish any one for conduct of which He was Himself the author and instigator; and therefore He could not punish Pharao for hardening his heart, if He had willed him to do so.

But in addition to the foregoing arguments, the facts of the case themselves prove clearly that the hardening of his heart was a voluntary act on Pharao's part, and by no means attributable to God; they go further, and prove that God not only did not will this hardness, but used miraculous agency to open the eyes of Pharao to see the extent of His power, and sought by the infliction of heavy chastisements to bring about his conversion, and win him from his obstinacy. In point of fact, does not the mere consideration of Pharao's pride and arrogance, audaciously declaring, as he did, that he would not recognize, much less obey the God of the Hebrews, and heaping, as he did, fresh burthens on that already oppressed and overburthened people in contempt of their God, make it quite clear that God desired his conversion? Did not the prodigies, which at last forced Pharao to humble himself before Moses and Aaron, and entreat their prayers on his behalf, that the God Whom he had proudly despised would deliver him from the plagues which afflicted him; nay, more, which forced him to confess his sin, and recognize at once the justice and equity of God, and his own impiety;[9] did not, I say,

---

[7] "Because thou wilt not let My people go" (Exodus x. 3, 4, and elsewhere).

[8] Lib. i. *Ad Monim.* cap. ii.

[9] "Pray ye to the Lord to take away the frogs from me" (Exodus viii. 8). "I have sinned also this time. The Lord is just: I and my people are wicked" (ix. 27).

these prodigies of themselves manifest God's desire for his conversion? So far, indeed, did Pharao humble himself, that he confessed he was guilty, not only against God, but also against those whom he regarded as his slaves. "I have sinned," said he to Moses and Aaron, "against the Lord your God and against you."[10]

Were not the heavy chastisements, miraculously inflicted on Pharao, the cause of his change of tone, and the gradual lowering of his pride, as is manifest by his concessions, first that only the heads of families might go, then that the old and the very young might accompany them, and finally that the whole multitude of the people with their flocks and herds and all other their possessions might depart? Is it not plain from this that the miracles, so far from hardening, served to melt him and soften his obstinacy?

This further remark, as St. Augustine observes,[11] remains to be added, namely, that if we regard the story of Pharao from the proper stand-point of God viewed as a Being infinitely good, we cannot fail to reckon these chastisements as so many manifestations of mercy on the part of God towards Pharao and the Egyptians. In fact God did far more than was necessary on His part to manifest to Pharao and the Egyptians His omnipotence by prodigies, His justice by chastisement, and His goodness by threats of punishment and warnings, which indicated a desire on His part that their conversion and submission might enable Him to dispense with severity. His patience was shown by the length of time

---

[10] Exodus x. 16.

[11] "If we regard God as we ought, we shall conclude that He did not shut Pharao out from His mercy. Might he not, just as he yielded under the pressure of chastisement, and sent the Hebrew people forth, also have been moved by the miracles to acknowledge a God Who displayed such power" (Lib. *De Præd. et Grat.* cap. xiv.).

during which He bore with Pharao's obstinacy, and the gradual progression of his punishment, whereby time was given to the King for repentance; and lastly His mercy appeared by delivering Pharao from the plagues the moment he bowed down before Him in obedience.

In conclusion, so good was God, that although obliged to punish the Egyptians, He so ordered His punishments as to make them instinct with profit, by manifesting thereby the falseness of their gods, and His own power and Divinity shown forth in the stupendous prodigies He performed.[12]

"Let no one therefore," sums up St. Augustine, "dare to impeach the justice of God, as do the pagans and Manichæans, but let all hold firmly the belief, that not the resistless power of God, but his own wickedness and stubborn pride thus over and over again hardened the heart of Pharao against the Divine command.[13] As it was, Pharao often bowed before the severity of his punishment and promised obedience, but as often retracted, moved either by ambition, which prompted him to retain his rule over a numerous people, or by avarice, which endeared to him the fruits of their toil and labour, or by pride and arrogance, which would not allow him to submit himself to the God of his own slaves, to acknowledge Him as his own God and to defer to His commands.[14]

---

[12] "And the Egyptians shall know that I am the Lord" (Exodus vii. 5; xiv. 6, 18).

[13] "Let no one therefore, with the pagans and Manichæans, presume to impeach the justice of God. But let each one be assured that Pharao was hardened so often against the commands of God by his own iniquity and indomitable pride, and not by the forcible constraint of God" (Serm. xxi. *In Appd.* n. 4).

[14] "Who is the Lord that I should hear His voice and let Israel go? I know not the Lord, neither will I let Israel go" (Exodus v. 2).

Pharao, instead of being grateful to God for the goodness, mercy, and forbearance, exercised in his behalf, acted like the spoiled child who abuses the kindness shown him, and grows hardened under chastisement.[15] God at last provoked by his obstinate persistence in persecuting the people of Israel, and justly incensed by his headlong effrontery and indomitable pride, overthrew and whelmed him beneath the waves. But in the very act of doing so, and of inflicting on him a punishment terrible in its severity, he gave him an opportunity of repenting of his obstinacy and hardness, of acknowledging the true God, and asking pardon for his sins; for at the first He only overturned the chariots of Pharao's army, and on the latter attempting to fly overwhelmed them in the waters.[16] It may also be remarked that death by drowning is not instantaneous, and consequently, as Pharao was the last to die, he had, as Cornelius à Lapide remarks,[17] time to repent and rescue himself from eternal, though not from temporal, death.

SECOND DIFFICULTY.—Is it not also very plain that God Himself blinds the eyes of the sinner in order that he may not be converted? The command of God delivered to the Prophet Isaias is sufficient to carry conviction on this point : " Blind," so runs the mandate, "blind the heart of this people [that of Israel], make their ears heavy and shut their eyes; lest they see with their eyes, and hear with their ears, and understand with their hearts, and be converted, and I heal them." And when the Prophet inquired, "how long, O Lord?" the

[15] "Pharao seeing that rest was given, hardened his own heart" (Exodus viii. 15).

[16] "He overthrew the wheels of the chariots, . . . and as the Egyptians were fleeing away, the waters came upon them, and the Lord shut them up in the middle of the waves" (Exodus xiv. 25, 27).

[17] *In Exod.* xiv. 24.

Solution of Difficulties.   37

answer was, "until the cities be wasted and without inhabitants, and the houses without men, and the land be left desolate."[18]

Answer.—It is perfectly absurd to take this text literally; for so understood, it would in the first place make God command the Hebrews to sin, in so far as He would be commanding them to disregard and be deaf to His commands; as we have already seen, when discussing the question of Pharao's hardness of heart. This text should not be so understood, in the second place, because it is contrary to common sense to suppose that God would send a prophet on a mission to blind His people, and thus hinder their conversion, a part opposed to the essential mission and function of a prophet. For remember that the Prophet's special function and mission is to communicate to the people the commands of God which they are to execute, or to forewarn the people of future events, in order that being converted from their sins they may avert threatened punishment, or being taught by the accomplishment of his predictions, may acknowledge their Divine origin, and listen to the teachings of those who uttered them.

It is therefore manifest that this prophecy of Isaias was a prediction of future events, and not a command of God, conveyed to His people. If proof of this view were wanting, we find it in the commentaries on Holy Writ of Cornelius à Lapide, Tirinus, Menochius, and Martini, who, adopting the reading in the Septuagint version, all agree that instead of the imperative mood,

[18] "Hearing, hear and understand not, and see the vision and know it not. Blind the heart of this people, and make their ears heavy, and shut their eyes, lest they see with their eyes, and hear with their ears, and understand with their heart, and be converted, and I heal them. And I said, How long, O Lord? And He said, Until the cities be wasted without inhabitant, and the houses without man, and the land shall be left desolate" (Isaias vi. 9—11).

the future tense of the indicative mood should be inserted in this prophecy. So altered, the context would run thus, *Audietis et videbitis, et non voletis intelligere et cognoscere*—"You shall hear and shall see, and will not understand and know." St. Basil, St. John Chrysostom, St. Cyril, and St. Jerome have adopted this reading, and accordingly thus paraphrase the original, "I know, O ye people of Juda, that you are all anxiously waiting the coming of the promised Messias; when He comes, however, you will reject Him. You shall hear His words and see His miracles, but you will not acknowledge them or believe them to be the works and miracles of the Messias. Nay, you will go farther, and charge Him with casting out devils in the name of Beelzebub."

In fact this passage is more than once quoted in the New Testament, and on every occasion it is referred to as a prophecy which shall have obtained its fufilment in the time of Jesus Christ, and on every occasion the future indicative is used instead of the imperative, as we above observed it ought to be. Moreover it is especially noteworthy the Lord Jesus does not say, that He spoke to the Jews in parables, "*in order* that seeing they *might not see*," &c., but "*because* seeing they do not see."[19] Hence it is made quite apparent by these texts from the New Testament that this prophecy conveyed, not a command, but a prediction.

In addition it may be observed with reference to the

---

[19] "Therefore do I speak to them in parables, because seeing they see not, and hearing they hear not, neither do they understand. And the prophecy of Isaias is fulfilled in them, who saith: By hearing you shall hear, and shall not understand, and seeing you shall see and not perceive" (St. Matt. xiii. 13, 14). "Well did the Holy Ghost speak to our Fathers by Isaias the Prophet: Go to this people and say to them, With the ear you shall hear and not understand, and seeing you shall see and shall not perceive" (Acts xxviii. 25, 26).

Solution of Difficulties. 39

tenth verse of the above passage from Isaias—a remark made also by St. John Damascene,[20] that it is customary in Holy Writ to give the name of action to the mere sufferance accorded by God, as we have before shown in the instance of Pharao's hardness of heart;[21] and just as the gloss upon that passage explains the words, "I will harden Pharao's heart" to mean "I will suffer it to be hardened," so here the words, "Blind the heart of this people," should be held to mean "Suffer their hearts to be blinded."[22]

The most obvious meaning of the passage in question is the following, which has been attached to it by Bergier: "Go and tell this people, you shall hear and you will not understand; you shall see and you will not know. Suffer them then to harden their hearts, to stop their ears, and to shut their eyes for fear of their seeing and understanding, of their being converted and healed, until the very weight of their wretchedness forces them to reconsider their condition." These are the plaintive accents of a Father compelled to punish

---

[20] Bk. iv.

[21] Exodus v. 22.

[22] It is observed by St. Augustine "that every language has its own peculiar phrases and turns of expression, which make nonsense when literally translated into a foreign tongue" (*De verit. Relig.* n. 49). Moreover, the same word has often many different meanings in the same language; for instance, the Latin word *ut* has eighteen different meanings attached to it in the Della Crusca Dictionary, of which it is enough to give two instances taken from Cicero, who employs the phrase "*ut* illud cogitares" in the sense of "*although* thou shouldst think so," and "*ut* non dedeceat" in the sense of "*in such sort that* it may not be unbecoming." In a word, it would take too long time and space to enumerate all the meanings of which the Latin particle *ut* is susceptible. We may therefore safely conclude that our proper course is to take words in that sense which shall produce an agreement with other texts, and not in one which shall lead merely to absurdity and contradiction.

a wayward child in order to his being brought to a better frame of mind and his eventual reform.

What more? Jesus Christ Himself solves the difficulty by the distinct assurance that the passage from Isaias vi. 9, 10, had a prophetic reference to the blindness shown by the Jews in rejecting His doctrine, and that this blindness was on their part altogether voluntary. We cannot do better than examine for ourselves His very words as recorded by St. Matthew: "Therefore do I speak to them in parables, *because*"—mark well that He does not say *in order that*—"seeing they see not, and hearing they hear not, neither do they understand." And in them is fulfilled the prophecy of Isaias, who saith: "By hearing you shall hear and shall not understand, and seeing you shall see and shall not perceive. For the heart of this people is grown gross, and with their ears they have been dull of hearing, and their eyes they have shut, lest at any time they should see with their eyes, and hear with their ears, and understand with their hearts, and be converted, and I should heal them."[23]

Now, in the first place, Jesus Christ assigns as the precise reason for His speaking to them in parables *because* they see not, hear not, and do not understand. Hence it appears that the motive of Jesus Christ in addressing them in parables was to rouse their attention and excite their curiosity in a more than ordinary degree. For it was to be expected that like the disciples they would require explanations, and thus afford Him an opportunity of explaining to them His doctrines. To say, therefore, that Jesus Christ spoke in parables to the Hebrew people, with a view to blind their eyes and harden their hearts, would be to do Him the foulest wrong.

[23] St. Matt. xiii. 13—15.

Solution of Difficulties. 41

It should also be observed that a taste for parables, and the use of figurative language, was common among all Eastern peoples. And hence our Divine Redeemer, adapting Himself to their custom, spoke to the people in parables.[24] He had other reasons besides, all worthy of His wisdom and goodness, for addressing them in this form of speech. And these were, first, because this style of speaking was best suited to the genius of the people, and best calculated to win Him a hearing, aud convey the full import of the sublime doctrine He wished to inculcate. Secondly, because the Scribes and Pharisees who sought to catch hold of His words were generally among His auditors;[25] and He therefore conveyed to them truths, necessary to be known, in the form of parables, which left no door open to their charges; besides, the parable did not ostentatiously hold up their vices to the popular gaze, and He thereby was enabled, out of consideration for their position, to screen their reputation. Thirdly, because, whilst He could thereby unfold all that was needed for instruction, He was enabled to throw a veil over whatever He purposed to withhold, until it should be revealed on the coming of the Holy Ghost. "You are not yet advanced enough to understand all," so spoke the Divine Redeemer to the Apostles themselves, " but when the Holy Ghost shall come, He will teach you everything without concealment or disguise."[26]

THIRD DIFFICULTY.—But surely, on the other hand, St. John distinctly says: "They [the Hebrews] could

---

[24] "And without parables He spoke not to them" (St. Matt. xiii. 34).

[25] St. Matt. xxii. 15.

[26] "He will teach you all truth. . . . What things soever He shall hear He shall speak" (St. John xvi. 13). "All things . . . I have made known to you" (St. John xv. 15).

not believe, because Isaias said again, *He hath blinded their eyes and hardened their hearts.*" [27]

Answer.—St. Augustine gives this answer: "They could not believe because *they would not*, and God, foreknowing the corruption of their will, foretold it by His prophet." [28] We have here, as a learned author observes, only a common mode of expressing our ideas. We say, for instance, of a person that he cannot make up his mind to a given course of action, when we mean to convey that he is prevented by his his own stubborn will from pursuing it. So, too, it was said of the Jews that they could not bring their minds to believe and accept the doctrine of Jesus Christ, when they were prevented by their pride from acknowledging Him as the Messias. [29]

St. Augustine, continuing his commentary on this text, in his controversy with the Pelagians, as reported in Mattei's *History of Theology*, page 23, goes on to say: "They, who in their pride attribute so much power to the human will, as enables men to dispense with the Divine aid in order to a good life, cannot possibly believe in Christ." And applying this reasoning to the Jews, he proceeds to say: "That they, too, by reason of this mental obliquity were unable to believe. Not that men are incapable of changing from bad to good, but that so long as they adhere to this opinion, belief is out of the question." [30] And here we may remark that

---

[27] St. John xii. 39, 40.

[28] "If I am asked why they could not, I at once answer because they would not. For God foresaw their evil will, and foretold it by His prophet" (Tract. liii. *In Joan.* nn. 6, 9).

[29] See Bergier, Diction. mot. *Aveuglement*, p. 155.

[30] "Those who are so puffed up with pride as to suppose their own will to be endowed with sufficient strength to enable them to dispense with the Divine assistance in order to live well, cannot believe in Christ. Hence, too, this people were unable to believe,

when St. Augustine says men can change, but not, so long as they adhere to this impious opinion emanating from pride, he again says in so many words, that they cannot, because they will not.

In proof that they, who become humble and put aside all preconceived notions to the prejudice of Jesus Christ, are capable of believing, we may with advantage turn to the same chapter of St. John, wherein the Evangelist, after at verse 39 saying "they could not believe," and at verse 40, that God had "blinded their eyes and hardened their hearts," subjoins at verse 42, "that many of the chief men [either of the nation or the Pharisees] also believed in Him, but because of the Pharisees they did not confess Him, that they might not be cast out of the synagogue."[31] A similar account is given of the preaching of St. Paul, with respect to whom we are told, that "some believed the things that were said; but some believed not."[32] The same fate befell these incredulous ones, who "loved the glory of men more than the glory of God,"[33] as, according to the Apostles, befell the false philosophers, that is to say, their heart became darkened, "for having known God, they did not glorify Him as God, and so were inexcusable."[34] St. Paul does not in this passage attribute their blindness to God, but to the passions which they made their gods.[35]

---

not because men are incapable of changing from bad to good, but because so long as they adhere to such an opinion, they cannot believe" (Tract. xii. *In Joan.* n. 10).

[31] St. John xii. 42.
[32] Acts xxviii. 24.
[33] St. John xii. 43.
[34] Rom. i. 20, 21.
[35] "In whom the god of this world hath blinded the minds of unbelievers, that the light of the Gospel of the glory of Christ, Who is the image of God, should not shine unto them" (2 Cor. iv. 4).

Jesus Christ, then, came into the world not to darken but to enlighten it by His heavenly teaching;[36] nor did He exclude from His light a single individual, no not even those who were blinded by their own malice."[37]

If we conclude that this blindness and hardness of heart takes place by God's permission, signified either by His abandonment of such unbelievers as He foresees will prove obstinate in unbelief, as St. Irenæus told the Maronites when they misapplied the passage in question, in other words, by His withdrawal from them and suffering them to remain in the darkness which they themselves have chosen;[38] or, as St. Augustine says,[39] by His withdrawing His aid from those who deem they need it not, we must limit our conclusions by two conditions. First, we must also say with St. Augustine, that these persons deserved to be blinded, with the permission of God, in punishment of some sin.[40] And, secondly, we must not suppose that the sinner in consequence of this blindness is altogether bereft of the means necessary for his conversion. On this head we may again quote the authority of St. Augustine, who, referring to the instance of Pharao,[41] points out that capable as he was of yielding after he had been visited by the whole of the ten plagues, he was capable also of yielding after the infliction of the

---

[36] "That was the true light, which enlighteneth every man that cometh into this world" (St. John i. 9).

[37] "Their own malice blinded them" (Wisdom ii. 21).

[38] "Men loved darkness rather than the light" (St. John iii. 19).

[39] "Hence they are blinded and their hearts hardened, because as they deny the necessity for Divine aid, they are not aided" (Tract. xii. *In Joan.* n. 10).

[40] "We are compelled to admit that they deserved to be blinded as a punishment for sins committed by them" (*In Matt.* quæst. 14).

[41] *Enarr. in Psalm.* vi. n. 8.

first.⁴² Indeed, as we observed in speaking of Pharao's hardness of heart, these plagues were inflicted on him with the object of softening his heart; and, though he afterwards relapsed into his original obstinacy, they for a time effected their object.

Furthermore it is to be observed that this blindness, whether it be the result of God's permission, or a punishment of sin, may perhaps be allowed to take its course because it is conducive to salvation.⁴³ Just as we often see among ourselves individuals, who turn a deaf ear to the warning voice of affection, allowed to suffer under some of the ills against which they were forewarned, not in consequence of any dislike towards them as individuals, but because it was the only way to wean them from evil courses and to make them in future amenable to advice. "Hence," concludes the Saint—and observe he this time lays down his proposition as an absolute truth—"we are to understand that God permitted their blindness, or allowed them to continue in it, with a view to their conversion."⁴⁴ We may therefore say with David: "It is good for us that Thou hast humbled us, because the motive for our chastisement, or being permitted to fall into sin was that, at our own expense, we might learn Thy justifications." ⁴⁵

⁴² "We must acknowledge that he could have acted in the same manner after he had been stricken by one of the plagues, as he did after he was stricken by the ten" (Serm. ii. *in Append.* 2, 3).

⁴³ "Consider whether we ought not to attribute what happened to them as a part of a remedy administered by the Divine mercy, so that as they were of a proud and stubborn will, the blindness with which they offended might be in proportion to the waywardness with which they followed after that blindness; and when thereby humbled, they might seek after the name of the Lord" (Tract. xii. *In Joan.* n. 11).

⁴⁴ "Whence we are to understand, that they were blinded in order that they might be converted" (*In Matt.* quæst. 14).

⁴⁵ "It is good for me that Thou hast humbled me, that I may learn Thy justifications" (Psalm cxviii. 71).

Let us, then, admire the infinite wisdom and goodness of God, Who out of the greatest evil is able and willing to bring forth our greatest good. Well, indeed, had the Jews deserved by their sins to be allowed to continue in their blindness. When Jesus Christ spoke to them in parables, they, as before observed, asked for no explanations, but under the influence of the mortal hatred they bore Him, and of anger at being rebuked for their vices, they went on adding to the blindness of their eyes and hardness of their hearts, affording a proof of the saying, that whoever holds another in hate dwells in darkness, and goeth he knoweth not whither.[46] Yet Jesus Christ not only made the blindness and hardness of heart of the Jews the instruments for working out our redemption, but, as the holy Doctor adds, He procured for these self-same blinded and hardened Jews themselves abundant lights for their conversion in the miracle of His Resurrection, the propagation of His holy Gospel, the preaching of the Apostles, and their numerous miracles.[47]

"Truly, O Lord, you have compassion on all, and shut your eyes to our sins in order that we may do penance.[48] And yet it is for the very reason of your being thus good in waiting for us that we abuse your mercy and proudly resist.[49] Nay, to such a height does our ingratitude reach, that we lay our transgressions at

[46] "He that hateth his brother is in darkness, . . . and knoweth not whither he goeth" (1 St. John ii. 11).

[47] "He told them of the judgments of God in the dim obscurity of parables, that after His Resurrection they might recur to them with the more saving repentance" (St. Augustine, *In Matt.* quæst. 14).

[48] "Thou hast mercy on all, because thou canst do all things, and overlookest the sins of men for the sake of repentance" (Wisd. xi. 24).

[49] "God hath given him place for penance, but he abuseth it in his pride" (Job xxiv. 23).

your door, saying with the people of Israel: 'Why hast Thou made us to err, O Lord, from Thy ways: why hast Thou hardened our hearts, that we should not fear Thee?'"[50] But no, says St. Augustine, God is not the cause of error and hardness of heart; the real cause is His patience which makes Him abstain from punishing sin, whilst He awaits the sinner's salvation.[51] For God acts towards us,[52] like the father who ceases to chastise his son whom he sees obstinately bent on evil courses, from apprehension of being provoked to inflict an injurious amount of punishment, and trusts that circumstances may arise to induce the lost one seriously to consider his position and reform his conduct.

Let us not then say: "Thou hast deceived me, O Lord,"[53] but let us rather confess our own ingratitude in despising the riches of God's goodness, patience, and long-suffering; and let us make up our minds now at last, once for all, to surrender at discretion, as we can no longer plead ignorance of the truth, that, out of His exceeding goodness, God has only our conversion in view.[54]

FOURTH DIFFICULTY.—Yet the answer given by Jesus Christ to His disciples, when they asked Him why He spoke to the multitudes in parables, is perfectly clear.

---

[50] Isaias lxiii. 17.

[51] "Not that God is the cause of our error and hardening, but that the patience with which He awaits our salvation, whilst He abstains from punishing delinquency seems to be the cause of error and hardness" (Serm. xxii. *in Append.* n. 5).

[52] "Whence God vehemently roused to anger, stayed His hand from striking" (*Ibid.*).

[53] Jer. xx. 7.

[54] "Despisest thou the riches of His goodness and patience and long-suffering? Knowest thou not that the benignity of God leadeth thee to penance?" (Rom. ii. 4.)

"Because," He said to them, "to you it is given to know the mysteries of the kingdom; but to them it is not given."[55] After which, He went on to explain the parable in detail to the disciples.

Answer.—The answer is that He spoke to the multitudes in parables for the reasons stated before in this chapter under the head of the second difficulty. It was not given to the multitude to understand His doctrine, because they closed their ears and shut their eyes, lest they should see and hear, and so recognize their evil plight, and be converted and cured of their wilful blindness.

For had they wished to profit by His teaching, they would have sought for an explanation when they failed to understand the parables; and Jesus Christ would have vouchsafed the explanation to them as He did to those who asked it at His hands.

It is true that we read in St. Mark: "To you it is given to know the mystery of the kingdom of God; but to them that are without, all things are done in parables, *that* seeing they may see and not perceive, and hearing they may hear and not understand"—*Ut videntes videant, et non videant; et audientis audiant, et non intelligant*;[56] but we must bear in mind our previous remarks on the meaning of the Latin particle *ut*, which must be here taken to signify *so that* or *in such manner that*, as it means in its original Greek equivalent.

In fact to suppose that Jesus Christ preached and taught and rebuked the Jews, in order that they should not hearken to Him and be converted, is to suppose an absurdity. Would it not be repugnant to the goodness and mercy of God as well as to the object with which He came into the world, namely, the sal-

---

[55] St. Matt. xiii. 11.
[56] St. Mark iv. 11, 12.

vation of sinners, who without Him would inevitably perish."[57]

Moreover, Jesus Christ Himself, as recorded by St. John, establishes the fact that the blindness of the Jews proceeded not from Him, but from their own wilful obstinacy: "For judgment," says He, "I am come into this world; that they who see not may see, and they who see may become blind. And some of the Pharisees who were with Him heard, and they said unto Him, are we also blind? And Jesus said unto them: if you were blind you should not have sin; but now you say we see, your sin remaineth."[58] He says further: "If I had not come and spoken to them, they would not have sin; but now they have no excuse for their sin."[59] It is therefore manifest that if their blindness had been caused, not by their own wilful obstinacy and pride, but by Jesus Christ, He would not, as He has done, have pronounced them culpable.

And let no one allege that the Hebrews would not have sinned, as by acting as they did they were fulfilling, as fulfil they needs must, the predictions of the Prophet. St. Augustine replies to such an allegation, that God in foretelling the future, predicted, but did not cause, the unbelief of the Jews, just as He cannot be said to cause the sins of men because He foreknows them.[60]

---

[57] "The Son of Man is come to seek and to save that which was lost" (St. Luke xix. 10).

[58] St. John ix. 39, seq.

[59] St. John xv. 22.

[60] "We answer that God in His foreknowledge predicted the unbelief of the Jews, yes He predicted, but did not cause it. For it cannot be said that because God has foreknowledge of sins, He therefore compels any one to sin" (Tract. lxiii. *In Joan.* n. 4).

CHAPTER IV.

Of the sense in which we are to understand God's abandonment of sinners and their reprobation.

FIRST DIFFICULTY.—Apparently it cannot be denied that there is a class of persons so utterly abandoned and rejected of God that the prayers and supplications of these unhappy ones are fruitless, since God no longer gives ear to them. Thus He takes away from them the possibility of salvation, whilst yet they are bound, under penalty of damnation, to hope to be saved. What assurance, in point of fact, can we have that we have not been abandoned by God in consequence of our resistance to grace, as we are told the city of Babylon was: "We would have cured Babylon," said the Lord, "but she is not healed; let us forsake her."[1] What peace can there be in such a state of hopeless uncertainty?

Answer.—In addition to the tranquillizing effect of that moral certainty which, as we observed in our second chapter, can be supplied from each man's conscience, by the assurance of his being in the state of grace, we have ample ground for believing, whatever may be our state, that we are not abandoned by God, and for confiding in God's mercy, provided we choose to avail ourselves of it. St. Thomas of Aquin, surnamed the Angelical Doctor, lays it down that Babylon and Israel are described as abandoned by their guardian angels, since the angels failed to ward off coming tribulations.[2] In like manner,

[1] Jer. li. 9.
[2] "Babylon and the house of Israel are said to be abandoned by their angels, because their angel guardians did not prevent their being subjected to tribulations" (P. i. q. 115, art. 1 ad 6).

according to the same authority, we are to put a similar construction on the expression, abandonment by God, which merely imports that God permits sinners to fall into tribulation and sometimes into sin, or does not prevent their doing so. Mgr. Martini quotes Origen and other writers in support of this interpretation; and hence he explains the word, "we would have saved Babylon," by the supposition that it was the nations subject to her who were speaking, and protesting that they had done all in their power to cure her, meaning thereby to defend her and rescue her from ruin. To conclude, St. Augustine lays down that God never abandons any one of His creatures, and that there is not a sinner, provided only that he have the use of reason, to whose heart God does not speak through the remorse of conscience; and he even denies that any sinner, however blinded and guilty, is in this life utterly bereft of Divine grace."[3] He says that God refused not His mercy to Pharao, as Pharao might have come to the knowledge of God from witnessing the mighty miracles whereby he was compelled to allow the people of Israel to depart.[4] Indeed, whenever, yielding to the inspiration of grace,[5] he repented

---

[3] "God never deserts any one made by Him; there is no soul, provided it be sane, to which God does not speak through conscience, and none so reprobate and blind as to be altogether shut out from the grace of God while life lasts. Such is blindness of the mind: whoever is consigned to it is separated from the interior light of God, though not altogether, as long as life lasts" (*Enarr. in Psalm.* vi. n. 8).

[4] "If we look upon God with the eyes of piety, we shall not deem that He refused mercy even to Pharao; for might not Pharao have recognized the infinite power of God on the evidence of His miracles, when he sent the people forth under the infliction of His scourge" (Lib. *De Præd. et Grat.* cap. xiv.).

[5] "I have sinned this time also. The Lord is just: I and my people are wicked.... And the thunders and the hail ceased" (Exodus ix. 27, 33, and elsewhere; viii. 28, 31; x. 16, 19).

and asked for pardon, God's wrath was at once appeased and His scourges withdrawn; until at last, provoked by his fiendish obstinacy in the relentless persecution of the Hebrew people, God caused both himself and his whole army to be swallowed up by the Red Sea.

God therefore has no other object in waiting for and bearing with sinners than to show them mercy,[6] and, as we have seen above, He never so abandons any one in life as to shut him out from repentance and salvation.

SECOND DIFFICULTY.—If we happened to have the misfortune of being of the class of reprobates to which the unhappy Esau, "who was hated by God,"[7] is recorded to have belonged, might we not well feel apprehension that God would show no more regard to our tears than to his?[8]

Meanwhile who can assure us that we do not belong to this class, and as long as uncertainty exists on this point, how can peace be found in the Christian religion which teaches this doctrine of despair?

Answer.—According to Cornelius à Lapide, Duhamel, Tirinus, and Menochius, the text from Malachy, properly understood, imports that God bore to Esau, not hatred, but a less degree of love than he did to Jacob. It should be understood, says Duhamel, as if the words were, "I have loved Esau less." These commentators go further, and say that, in this passage, Jacob and Esau should be taken as representatives of their respective descendants, and that the nature of the Lord's preference for one over the other is shown in the subsequent verses,

---

[6] "Therefore the Lord waiteth that He may have mercy on you" (Isaias xxx. 18).

[7] "I have loved Jacob, but have hated Esau" (Malach. i. 2, 3; Rom. ix. 13).

[8] "For he found no place for repentance, though with tears he had sought it" (Heb. xii. 17).

which may be read as follows: "I have shown My love to be greater for you, O children of Israel, than for the Idumæans, so far as regards the land wherein you dwell; for to you have I given a fertile land, abounding in fruits of every kind; but to them, on the contrary, I have given a barren land, and craggy and desolate mountains to be their dwelling-place. Moreover, you I have restored to the land of your nativity, them I have left in captivity; wherefore it shall be said of them: 'This is the people with whom the Lord is angry for ever: not indeed with the anger of reprobation from grace and glory, but with an anger that shall keep them for ever from regaining their native land, which shall remain a desert, and the abode of dragons;'[9] and this nation shall never more be known or distinguished from the other nations of the earth, but shall be confounded with other peoples.

St. Paul puts the same meaning on this passage, namely, that it imports the superiority of Jacob over Esau in power and worldly prosperity, when he says,[10] "for the elder shall serve the younger," according to the prophecy in Genesis, that the descendants of the twin brothers shall be divided, and that the younger shall overcome the elder.[11]

In the next place, Cornelius à Lapide observes with reference to the text of St. Peter which states "that Esau found no place for repentance although with tears he

---

[9] "The people with whom the Lord is angry for ever" (Malach. i. 4). That is (according to Cornelius à Lapide) the Idumæans are a people over whom the anger and vengeance of God shall brood for ever; for He will punish them with everlasting wasting, ruin, and desolation.

[10] Rom. ix. 12.

[11] "Two nations are in thy womb, and two peoples shall be divided out of thy womb. And one people shall overcome the other, and the elder shall serve the younger" (Gen. xxv. 23).

had sought it," that it is to be taken as having reference not to eternal reprobation either from grace or glory, but solely to the loss of his father's blessing, and therewith of the birthright which he had sold to his brother Jacob, as clearly appears from the very first words of the text in question, which are "when he desired to inherit the benediction."[12]

Bergier says[13] that the repentance of Esau could not cancel the special blessing bestowed by Isaac on Jacob, whereby he was as it were constituted the founder of the race from whom the Messias was to spring. Now this blessing was not a privilege of primogeniture, but a grace which God was pleased in the exercise of His discretion to confer on Jacob, as He foretold previously to the birth of the brothers that He would do. As for the rest, Esau was not even left without those temporal goods which His soul desired; for Isaac promised him the dews of heaven and the fruits of the earth, and his descendants were for a long time more powerful than those of Jacob. We gather from all this that Esau's rejection had reference solely to the determination of the Messias to be born, not from his race, but from that of Jacob, and that it has no connection whatever with eternal reprobation, rejection of repentance, or refusal of pardon. So far Bergier.

Others again, such as Theodoret, Theophylact, St. Anselm, as quoted by Cornelius à Lapide, St. John Chrysostom, and St. Thomas, as quoted by Mgr. Martini, hold that in the text of St. Paul, "he found no place for repentance," the word repentance refers to Esau, and the meaning is that God was heedless of his tears, and

[12] "For know ye that afterwards when he desired to inherit the benediction, he was rejected: for he found no place of repentance, although," &c. (Heb. xii. 17).

[13] *Tableau de la Miséricorde Divine*, p. 121. Edit. Besancon, 1871.

did not aid him to obtain pardon, in consequence of the imperfection of his repentance, which was the result of despair, and of rage and envy of his brother.[14] He repented, according to the Angelical Doctor and Cornelius à Lapide, not of having sold his birthright, but for having lost it. He repented not of the sin, but for the loss caused him by it[15]—a repentance such as is experienced by the damned in Hell.

Others again, also quoted by Cornelius à Lapide, understand the word repentance in this passage as referring to Isaac and not to Esau, a meaning to be deduced from the words of the Epistle of St. Paul, which according to this view imply that Esau was unable even by his tears to move his father to repent of having blessed Jacob, and to recall the blessing along with the inheritance it conferred. And in support of this construction we have the authority of St. Paul, who records that when Esau sought to inherit the blessing, his petition was rejected, although it was enforced by tears; thereby clearly implying that it was the loss of the blessing and not the desire of repentance which moved Esau to tears.[16]

THIRD DIFFICULTY. — Antiochus "prayed to the Lord, of Whom he was not to obtain mercy."[17] Therefore, notwithstanding God's manifold promises to hear

[14] "Wherefore neither did Esau obtain pardon, for he sought it not in the manner that he ought; for his tears were not the result of repentance, but of his trial and his wrath" (St. Chrysostom, Hom. viii. *Ad Pop. Antioch.*).

[15] Cornelius à Lapide, *In Epist. ad Heb.* xii. 19, and M. Martini.

[16] "For know that even after desiring to gain the blessing, he was rejected, for he found not a place for repentance, although he sought for it [the blessing] with tears" (as Cornelius à Lapide translates in the place cited).

[17] "The wicked man prayed to the Lord, of Whom he was not to obtain mercy" (2 Machab. ix. 13).

and pardon us, here is a case where recourse to Him was useless. How then can we, with the example of Antiochus before our eyes, trust in God's promises and hope in Him without fear of being rejected.

Answer.—Tirinus and Menochius, as well as the context itself, show us that although Antiochus prayed the Lord to deliver him from the dreadful calamities he saw impending over him, he felt no repentance for the enormities which he well knew he had committed in Jerusalem.[18] Impatient under his sufferings, and rendered insupportable to himself by his own stench, he prayed for, but obtained not from the Lord, the wished-for cure; and in his despair under his terrible and unintermittent sufferings, he wrote to the Jews in the confident hope that through their intercession his cure would be effected. His letter concludes with a solemn falsehood, namely, with an invitation and prayer to the Jews to remain faithful to him and to his son, out of consideration for the many benefits, both public and private, which he claimed he had conferred on them. The fact being, that he had invariably maltreated and persecuted the Jews, and that the very object with which he had undertaken the journey on which he was then engaged, was to convert all Jerusalem into one common grave by the indiscriminate slaughter of all the inhabitants.[19] Hence

[18] "But now I remember the evils I have done in Jerusalem. . . . I know therefore that for this cause these evils have found me; and behold I perish with great grief in a strange land" (1 Machab. vi. 12, 13).

[19] "And when he himself could not now abide his own stench, . . . Then this wicked man prayed to the Lord, of whom he was not to obtain mercy. But his pain not ceasing, despairing he wrote to the Jews: Having great hope to escape my sickness, I pray you and request of you that remembering favours both public and private, you will every man of you continue faithful to me and my son. . . . He had spoken so proudly that he would come to Jerusalem and make it a common burying-place of the Jews" (2 Mach. ix. 12, 13, 18, 22, 26, 4).

it is that the Scripture, as Tirinus observes, emphatically says: "This wicked man prayed;" signifying thereby that his heart was in nowise changed, but that he was still interiorly the same man of wickedness, a deceiver and hypocrite in all his words and acts. On the other hand, had Antiochus appealed to God with a contrite and humble heart,[20] God might possibly have been moved to pity and have delivered him from his sufferings, as He did in the case of Manasses, the wicked King of Judæa. This King, you will remember, was, owing to his many iniquities and scandalous life, stripped of his kingdom, and led captive to Babylon; when, he no sooner found himself consigned to the dark vaults of a dungeon, and loaded with fetters, than he turned to the Lord with all his heart. Whereupon, scarcely had he implored the Lord to exercise His infinite mercy in his behalf, than he was restored to liberty and re-established in his kingdom.[21]

Had Antiochus acted as Manasses did, although it might not have pleased God to deliver him from temporal punishment, He would most assuredly have pardoned him his sins, as He pardoned the sins of David.[22] For even when God in His anger wills the punishment of sinners in this life, His anger is nevertheless at once appeased, and He pardons their sins, provided they bow before the might of His arm, and with a contrite and humble heart sue to be forgiven;[23] nay more, He makes

---

[20] "A contrite and humble heart, O God, Thou wilt not despise" (Psalm l. 19).

[21] "And after that he was in distress he prayed to the Lord, and did penance exceedingly before God; . . . and He heard his prayer and brought him again to Jerusalem with his kingdom" (2 Paralip. xxxiii. 12, 13).

[22] "The sword shall never depart from thy house. . . . The Lord also hath taken away thy sin" (2 Kings xii. 10, 13).

[23] "Who when thou hast been angry, wilt show mercy, and in the time of tribulation forgiveth the sins of them that call on Thee" (Tobias iii. 13).

their very chastisement an instrument of eternal salvation, not only to the sufferers, but to others whom the spectacle of retributive justice strikes with terror, and causes carefully to avoid a course attended by such fatal consequences.[24]

In conclusion, there is no doubt, says Bergier, that God did not work the miracle of restoring Antiochus to health and life. He therefore died of his sickness, and in this sense failed to obtain the mercy he sued for; but as to the question whether he did or did not obtain from God the pardon of his sins the sacred historian does not inform us.[25]

FOURTH DIFFICULTY.—On the other hand Isaias seems clearly enough to point out the cause of the abandonment of the sinner and his rejection by God in the passage where he says, "That although the Lord is able to pardon and save sinners, yet their iniquities interpose such a barrier, that He no longer views them with an eye of kindness, and no longer hearkens to them."[26] Who knows whether we be not in this predicament?

Answer.—Cornelius à Lapide and Tirinus, in their summary of the chapter of Isaias from which the above quotation is taken, declare—as indeed is perfectly clear from the whole chapter and from the chapter preceding —that the subject treated of therein more particularly relates to temporal evils, from which God refused to deliver the sufferers, because, as He desired their good and correction, He willed that they should endure the

---

[24] "Not for the destruction but the correction of our nation" (2 Machab. vi. 12).

[25] Bergier, *Tabl. de la Miser. Div.* p. 120.

[26] "Behold the hand of the Lord is not shortened that it cannot save, but your iniquities and your sins have hid His face from you, that He should not hear" (Isaias lix. 1, 2).

Solution of Difficulties. 59

temporal punishment due to their sins. Cornelius à Lapide adds that God in this instance evidently inflicts punishment against His own inclination, and therefore that it cannot be thence inferred that God ever abandons the sinner, or will refuse to hearken to his cry for pardon, or to any of his prayers relating to eternal salvation.

FIFTH DIFFICULTY.—But does not Jesus Christ utter this precise threat against sinners when He says, "You shall seek Me and shall not find Me . . . and therefore you shall die in your sin."[27] How can this utterance be reconciled with the promise of pardon to the sinner at what hour soever he shall seek it with a contrite and humble heart?

Answer.—This difficulty is solved by a few words spoken in obedience to God's command by the Prophet Jeremias to the Hebrew people: "You shall seek Me and shall find Me," declares the prophet, "when you shall seek Me with all your heart."[28]

The reason therefore why Jesus Christ told the Jews that they should seek Him and not find Him, but should die in their sins, was because He knew they would not seek Him with that humble and contrite heart which, as we learn from David, God never despises.[29] No! He knew that they would seek Him in their hate with the design of persecuting Him in His own person, or in that of His disciples, and not with a view of being converted and embracing the Gospel truths; on which account St. Augustine thus paraphrases our Lord's words, "You shall seek Me from motives of hatred, and not of love."[30]

---

[27] St. John vii. 34; viii. 21.
[28] Jer. xxix. 13.
[29] "A contrite and humble heart, O God! Thou wilt not despise" (Psalm l. 19).
[30] Hom. *in Evang. Joan.* See St. John vii. 1, 20, 25, 30, 32.

If we wanted proof of this view we find it in the Gospel of St. John, where we read that the Jews sought an opportunity to arrest Him and take His life, which caused Jesus to say to them, "Yet a little while I am with you, and then I go to Him that sent Me,"[31] and further on, "You shall seek Me and shall not find Me; and where I am thither you cannot come."[32] Finally, after repeating the last cited words, He adds: "and you shall die in your sin;"[33] and because they had not as yet been informed why it was that they should seek without finding Him, and should not be able to go whither He went, He thus explained the reason: "therefore I said to you that you shall die in your sins; for if you believe not that I am He you shall die in your sins."[34]

SIXTH DIFFICULTY.—In vain do you attempt to reconcile the infinite goodness of God with the idea of Him presented by the Christian religion. In fact, religion teaches us that God, so far from being inclined to show mercy to sinners, will, in punishment of their obstinacy, be deaf to their cries when in the throes of death they shall call on Him, yea, and even will laugh at them, and mock them in their agony, and will have no regard to their prayers, which shall be an abomination and an execration unto Him.[35] If, as appears from

[31] St. John vii. 33.
[32] St. John vii. 34.
[33] St. John viii. 21.
[34] St. John viii. 24.
[35] "Because I called and you refused. . . . I also will laugh in your destruction, and will mock when that which you feared has come upon you" (Prov. i. 24, 26). "Then shall they call on Me and I will not hear: they shall rise in the morning and shall not find Me" (Prov. i. 28). "He that turneth away his ears from hearing the law, his prayer shall be an abomination" (Prov. xxviii. 9). "The victims of the wicked are an abomination to the Lord" (Prov. xv. 8).

the above quotations, such be the case, how can any one believe, much less hope in a God, Who is so profuse in the most solemn promises to the sinner of pardon of all his sins without exception,[36] so long as life endures, all for the purpose of laughing at the repentant sinner, and turning him into ridicule when he sues for pardon? Who can harbour a particle of love for a God Who, proclaiming Himself to be all goodness and mercy, and gentler than the most loving of mothers, feels the while less pity for the sorrows of His children than wild animals exhibit for their young?

Answer.—Grievous indeed would be the wrongs done to God if we framed to ourselves such an injurious and distorted idea of Him, or deemed that views such as these embodied the doctrine of the Catholic Church. That they do not and cannot do. To come to the solution of the difficulty—it is to be observed that of all the various meanings assigned for the Latin word *Interitus* by the numerous authors whom Cornelius à Lapide cites, the most obvious and natural seems to be either the rendering of the Septuagint, where *in interitu* is expressed by a phrase equivalent to *in perditione* (in destruction), or the explanation of Symmachus, who says that God being ever and always a lover of order, as shown forth in the fitness of things, rejoices to see all things settled in their proper places, the proper place of the justified being Heaven, and of the damned Hell.

The text in question therefore must be taken to mean that the moment the sinner ceases to breathe—for while life lasts he cannot be said to be in death—his tears shall no longer produce any effect upon God, for he has

---

[36] "The wickedness of the wicked shall not hurt him, in what day soever he shall turn from his wickedness" (Ezech. xxxiii. 12). "I will not remember all his iniquities that he hath done" (Ezech. xviii. 22).

ceased to be a wayfarer, and has reached his journey's end, where compassion has no place, and his sentence becomes irreversible.

Furthermore, if the verse be considered in its entirety, it will be found to bear out the explanation given of it by St. Bernard. . In substance the Scripture says, "Because I called, and you would not come, yea, even despised and laughed at all my suggestions for your good, so long as you lived, I, when you are dead, will in turn have no regard to your groans or your woes; in other words, when that shall come to you which you feared." [37] And do sinners fear anything more than that death which shall end their pleasures, strip them bare of riches, and send them headlong to Hell?

The verse which follows the one in question adds further confirmation to this view. It may be thus rendered: "When calamity shall already have come, and spent its sudden fury upon you, and when death as a raging tempest shall have overtaken you." [38] Note that the language of the Scripture is not "when calamity shall come," but "when *calamity shall already have come*," being thus expressed in the past future.

On the other hand, Cornelius à Lapide, Menochius, and Mgr. Martini hold that the Latin word *interitus* means death or destruction, and that the passage, where it occurs, signifies that God will laugh at sinners after death. Not indeed, as St. Gregory remarks, that God is capable of mocking any one, but that He will no longer exercise clemency or compassion on behalf of sinners

---

[37] "Because I called and you refused. . . . You despised all My counsel. . . . I also will laugh in your *destruction* [in *interitu vestro*], and will mock when that shall come to you which you feared" (Prov. i. 24—26).

[38] "When sudden calamity shall fall on you, and *destruction* (*interitus*), as a tempest shall be at hand: when tribulation and distress shall come upon you" (Prov. i. 27).

after death,[39] and will show how truly ridiculous are they who prefer temporal to eternal good. Hence these interpreters translate the Latin words: *cum vobis id, quod timebatis, advenerit* by the English, "when death"—the only thing feared by the wicked—"shall have come upon you."

Cajetan, as quoted by Cornelius à Lapide, adopts the same interpretation of this passage, and Venerable Bede explains it to allude to the innumerable evils which shall befall the damned on the Day of Judgment, and the stinging reproaches they shall hear from the lips of their Divine Judge.

But even although we understand the text to mean that God would no longer exercise mercy towards sinners, or be moved to pity by their groans after they had allowed themselves to be overtaken by His terrible chastisements, still the words can only be understood as referring to temporal evils. In which case the passage should be rendered thus: "God will not give ear to their prayers for deliverance from these temporal chastisements, but will continue to desire their punishment, as they refused to listen to His counsels." That this is the correct interpretation appears clearly from the twenty-seventh verse, where the evils with which the sinner is threatened are enumerated, as well as from the thirty-third verse, where the blessings promised to those who hearken to the counsels of God[40] are set forth. To all which this further observation is to be added, that the words were here addressed to the Hebrew people, whom He ever sought to keep steadfast in the observance of

---

[39] "When God is said to laugh at human affliction, the meaning is, that He will not have pity on it; therefore when He says, 'I will laugh in your destruction," He in effect says, I will not be moved by pity to compassionate your afflictions" (9 *Moral.* cap. xx.).

[40] "But he that shall hear Me, shall rest without terror, and shall enjoy abundance without fear of evils" (Prov. i. 33).

His holy law by the threat of temporal punishment in case of disobedience, or the promise of temporal rewards in case of their fidelity.

The passage in question cannot, therefore, be understood as applying to their eternal reprobation; for so understood it would be in direct contradiction to the Divine promise conveyed through the Prophet Ezechiel,[41] to the effect that even after He had thundered forth the sentence of death against the wicked, He was ready to revoke that sentence of eternal death, and grant the wicked one his life, if he repented of his sins, learned to do good, and repaired, as far as he was able, the evil he had done.

Such also was evidently the opinion of the Angelical Doctor, who goes so far as to say that even if it were revealed to one that a sentence of eternal damnation had been passed against him, he could not accept it as final, not even for the purpose of conforming to the will of God; and further, that it would be sinful to assent to it, because God wills not the damnation of any one unless it be on account of sin, and therefore if one assented to his own damnation he would be conforming himself to the will not of God, but of sin. Nay, even in the case of the sinner, whose sin God foresees, and pronounces in consequence a sentence of damnation against him, such sinner should not accept that sentence if revealed to him, but look upon the revelation merely in the light of a threat, to be carried out only in the event of his persisting in sin.[42]

---

[41] "And if I shall say to the wicked, Thou shalt surely die; and he do penance for his sin and do judgment and justice . . . and restore the pledge, . . . he shall surely live, and shall not die" (Ezech. xxxiii. 14, 15).

[42] "Hence it would not be to conform to the will of God absolutely to assent to one's own damnation. It would be rather to conform to the will of sin" (St. Thomas, *De Verit.* q. 3, a. 8). "By way of threat" (*Ibid.*).

Solution of Difficulties. 65

Nor is there any limit as to time, for the promise is that in what day soever the sinner shall be converted, his wickedness, no matter how grievous or how manifold, shall not hurt him.[43] Hence St. Jerome and St. Ambrose rightly conclude, that no one ought to despair of salvation on account of past sins; and St. Ambrose adds the further reason that the Lord will recall the sentence of death if the sinner during life repents from his heart,[44] as He revoked the sentence pronounced against the Ninivites after it had been foretold to them by the Prophet Jonas, and granted them pardon.[45]

It is particularly worthy of remark that the reason assigned by the Prophet Jonas for having taken to flight, and failed to carry out the orders of the Lord was that he foresaw that the mercy and goodness of God would make void His threat[46] in case the Ninivites should repent, as indeed they did. For although the threat of destruction was unconditional in terms, yet the Prophet knew, and the Ninivites hoped, that in its true meaning it was otherwise; and in point of fact God did pardon them.[47]

The various explanatory reasonings hitherto urged are

---

[43] "The wickedness of the wicked shall not hurt him in what day soever he shall turn from his sin. . . . None of his sins which he hath committed shall be imputed to him" (Ezech. xxxii. 12, 16).

[44] "No one should despair of salvation who has been converted to a better way of life, since St. Matthew himself was suddenly changed from being a publican into an Apostle" (*Comm. in Matt.* lib. i. cap. i.) "God can change the sentence, if you manage to withdraw from offence" (*In Luc.* lib. ii. cap. i.).

[45] "Yet forty days and Ninive shall be destroyed. . . . And God had mercy, and He did it not" (Jonas iii. 4, 10).

[46] "Therefore I went before to flee, . . . for I know that Thou art a gracious and merciful God, patient and of much compassion, and easy to forgive evil" (Jonas iv. 2).

[47] "Who can tell if . . . God will forgive? And God had mercy, and He did it not" (Jonas iii. 9, 10).

F

applicable to the right interpretation of the twenty-eighth verse of the same chapter, where the words of the Lord are, "then they shall call upon Me, and I will not hear them." [48]

Consequently we may understand that "then" in this passage signifies—as Venerable Bede and Lyranus, as quoted by Cornelius à Lapide, interpret it—the Day of Judgment, or that their prayer to God would be only for deliverance from temporal evils, from which, as in the case of Antiochus, He would no longer exempt them; [49] or that they would not repent of their sins from their heart, according to the opinion of Mgr. Martini; or, finally, that although after the heartfelt repentance for their sins they should most assuredly obtain the remission of the eternal punishment due to them, they could not hope to be exempted, at least altogether, from temporal chastisement.[50] Therefore, when the class of wicked men here typified, on being sorely visited by calamity, arise and call on God to deliver them, they shall not find Him; in other words, He will no longer deliver them, but as they closed their ears against His warning voice bidding them repent, so will He be now inexorable in His punishment.

Finally, the Lord says, "He that turneth away his ears from hearing the law, his prayer shall be an abomination."[51] The following explanation of this verse

---

[48] Prov. i. 28.

[49] "For these wicked men call on God, and asked to be delivered not from their guilt, but from its penalty, death: therefore is their prayer not heard" (Cornelius à Lapide).

[50] "But although if they repented with heartfelt contrition . . . they should indubitably obtain remission of their guilt, yet not so of the punishment due to guilt, at least of the whole of it, . . . for God is inexorable in punishment, and He shuts His ears against the impenitent, because they had previously shut their ears against the voice of His warning" (Cornelius à Lapide).

[51] Prov. xxviii. 9.

is applicable also to Proverbs xv. 8, and to similar passages.

This verse, according to Cornelius à Lapide and Mgr. Martini, exemplifies God's treatment of those persons who, while they pray, continue wedded to evil, and hanker after sin. Note that the Lord's words are addressed to one who "turneth away his ears" at the very time when the Lord is speaking, and not to one who has turned or shall turn them away; to one, in fact, who apparently desired to make God Himself an associate in his sin. As well might a thief pray for a favourable opportunity to steal, or the would-be adulterer for the removal of obstacles to his impure designs, or a man call upon God, as St. Augustine puts the case, to rain down calamities on his enemy. St. Gregory says,[52] and the Angelical Doctor agrees with him,[53] that God so acts because the prayer which is founded in sin is an abomination. This observation, however, in no way applies to sinners who desire to withdraw from sin, and pray that God would enable them to amend their lives; for, as St. Augustine and St. Thomas (as quoted by Cornelius à Lapide) say, such as these are ever heard.

In fact, to say that a sinner praying from his heart that he may be converted shall not be heard, is to make out his condition to be worse than that of the damned themselves. They can sin no more, and consequently cannot add to their delinquency or their punishment; but the sinner, in the case supposed, debarred from conversion—as of himself he can do nothing, and God

[52] Hom. xxvii. on the Gospels.
[53] "If you pray for evil on your enemies, your prayer will be turned into sin" (Serm. lvi.). "If therefore the sinner when he asks for anything ... in furtherance of his sinful desire (suppose he were to ask God, for instance, to accomplish some sin), herein he is not heard by God out of mercy, though sometimes he may be out of vengeance" (q. 83, art. 15 ad 2, et art. 16 ad 1).

refuses to hear him—and yet capable of sinning continually, should be adding demerit to demerit, and consequently heaping damnation upon damnation. Moreover the sinner is enjoined by the command of God, under pain of damnation, to hope for salvation and the means of attaining it, yet in the case supposed, by placing this obligation on the sinner, and at the same time refusing to hear or help him, God would be cutting him off from all hope, and every resource, since the sinner is of himself incapable of effecting anything towards his eternal salvation.

Far from us be ideas so insulting to the goodness and mercy of God, and so much opposed to the doctrine of the Church! Not only is it not true, as we observed when discussing the first difficulty, that God ever abandons or rejects sinners, by refusing to provide them with the aids necessary [54] for their conversion and pardon, when they sue for it, but He actually makes them a distinct promise, through the mouth of the Prophet Zachary, that if they return to Him with contrite hearts they shall be to Him as dear as they were before He had cast them off.[55]

[54] See Tesoro, part i. p. 290 in fine et seq.
[55] "And I will bring them back again, . . . and they shall be as they were when I cast them off" (Zach. x. 6).

CHAPTER V.

On Lukewarmness.

FIRST DIFFICULTY.—How can we, sinners that we are, ever rid ourselves of a reasonable apprehension of being abandoned, seeing that our Lord requires of us to be holy and perfect like our Heavenly Father,[1] and goes so far as to protest that He will begin to vomit forth out of His mouth whoever shall not serve Him with the required fervour? "Because thou art lukewarm," was the threatening message sent by God to the Bishop of the Church of Laodicea, "I will begin to vomit thee out of My mouth."[2] Now who will presume to assure himself that he serves God with fervour, or that he is not in this lukewarm state? And is not such a state equivalent to abandonment by God, since it is the prelude to that loss of grace and light which will bring on a lassitude in our journey on the road of virtue, which lassitude in its turn, like a moral atrophy, is sure to result in death eternal?

Answer.—It is undoubtedly true that our Lord desires our holiness and perfection, and proposes the holiness and perfection of Himself and of His Heavenly Father as our pattern. But it is equally true that He does not require from us any higher degree of sanctity than our frail human nature, assisted by His grace, is capable of. The yoke of the Lord is sweet, and presses not heavily on the bearer; for He is a just God, and requires no impossibilities, nor anything too difficult to perform;

---
[1] "You shall be holy because I am holy" (1 St. Peter i. 16). "Be you perfect as also your Heavenly Father is perfect" (St. Matt. v. 48).
[2] Apoc. iii. 16.

because, says St. Augustine, God, Who is our Father, lays not on the children whom He loves any commands that are beyond endurance.³

Next comes the threat of abandonment held out to those who are lukewarm in the service of God. But, before discussing this part of the difficulty, let us examine what is meant by being lukewarm. Know then that the commentators on Holy Scripture, Cornelius à Lapide, Menochius, Duhamel, and Mgr. Martini, hold that the term lukewarm designates that class of men who are careful to avoid the grosser kinds of sins, and who, because they are not stained with guilt of the deepest dye,⁴ are blind enough to pride themselves on their innocence and on their imaginary wealth of virtue and merits.⁵

Menochius holds that the word lukewarm is used to designate those who believe themselves to be just, because they want courage deliberately to commit heinous offences, and who, caring little to attain any high degree of perfection or purity of life, become an easy prey to disorderly inclinations, and give themselves unbounded license within the range of sins not mortal.⁶

---

³ "God does not command impossibilities" (Trent. Sess. vi. cap. x.). "His commandments are not heavy" (1 St. John v. 3). "For My yoke is sweet and My burthen light" (St. Matt. xi. 30).

⁴ "For the lukewarm being unconscious of the more heinous kinds of sin, . . . pride themselves on their innocence and sanctity" (Cornelius à Lapide, cap. iii. v. 17).

⁵ "For the lukewarm is one who holding in contempt the rules of virtuous conduct, abstains indeed from the grosser sorts of vice, but leads an effeminate and torpid life" (Menoch. in v. 15, 16, *Ibid.*). "The lukewarm are those who deem themselves good because they abstain from great crimes."

⁶ "He is called lukewarm, who dares not offend God with malice prepense, and on that account deems himself to be just; but he neglects the cultivation of the purer and more perfect standard of life, whence he easily gives way to his concupiscences, and allows himself to commit any faults so long as they appear to him only venial" (Menoch. *Ibid.*).

Lastly, Bossuet, Duhamel, and Mgr. Martini[7] hold that the class of the lukewarm also comprises those who wish to serve two masters, Jesus Christ and the world, and can never decide on which side to range themselves.

Now as to the Bishop of Laodicea, by whose tepidity our Lord was so strongly moved; he prided himself on the possession of such abundant riches as placed him far beyond the reach of temporal needs[8]—for, as Cardinal Baronius remarks, on the authority of Tacitus, Strabo, and others, Laodicea was, in the year 62 of our era, an extremely wealthy city—and hence the Bishop became spiritually poor and lukewarm.

The generality of commentators, however, are of opinion that this Bishop was reduced to the most deplorable condition in consequence of his priding himself on his possession of spiritual gifts; and Mgr. Martini goes so far as to say that in this case tepidity was more harmful than open wickedness, on account of the pride and misplaced confidence which resulted from such a state of soul.

In reality he was, according to the message sent him by our Lord, "poor and blind and naked," and he was all this chiefly for three reasons. First, he was poor, because he lacked that ardent charity which is essential to the office of a bishop, who is under an obligation of being beyond reproach.[9]

---

[7] "The lukewarm, adhering to neither side, try to hold a middle course between the world and the Gospel" (Bossuet, *Comm. in Apoc.* iii. 16; Martini, *Ibid.* 15, 16).

[8] "Because thou sayest, I am rich and made wealthy, and have need of nothing" (Apoc. iii. 17). "In other words, by his gold and temporal possessions, for thereby he became poor and lukewarm in spiritual matters" (Cornelius à Lapide, *in Apoc.* iii. 17).

[9] "And knowest not that thou art wretched, and miserable, and poor and blind and naked" (Apoc. iii. 17). "Poor, because wanting charity" (Cornelius à Lapide, *Men. et altri*). See also P. Orasio, *De Parma Espos. Lett. e Mor.* t. i. "It behoveth therefore a bishop to be blameless" (1 Tim. iii. 2).

Secondly, he was blind, owing to his want of humility and his little consideration for the last things. Thus, being blinded by pride, he recognized not his poverty, but rather esteemed himself so rich in good works as to be independent of further aids to salvation. Accordingly the eye-salve wherewith the Lord recommends him to anoint his eyes meant humility and consideration of the last things.[10]

Thirdly, and lastly, he was naked, because, as his good works were vitiated by pride and hypocrisy, he was void of merit and of every virtue becoming his exalted state.[11]

Now say, was not the state of lukewarmness thus described a terrible condition for a bishop to find himself in?

Supposing even that he did not belong to the class of those who, because they have not committed heinous sins, are puffed up by a belief in their own goodness and a self-consciousness of their own innocence, though indeed, for the reasons just adduced, and also because he was styled "wretched and miserable and poor and blind," it is probable that he did belong to the above category; yet at any rate, did not his readiness to commit deliberately and with his eyes open every possible sin, provided it were not mortal, argue a disposition on his part to fall into mortal sin on the earliest occasion? Therefore our

---

[10] "And anoint thy eyes with eye-salve that thou mayest see" (Apoc. iii. 18). "Eye-salve means humility," says Rupertus: "purify thy heart with humility, that thou mayest see;" and it means also consideration of the last things: "by consideration cleanse the eye of thy mind, which is fixed on earth and thereby blinded" (so say Primas, Anselm, Richard, Hugo, Ritua, and Menochius).

[11] "Naked, because wanting in good works, and because he did all his actions in the spirit of over-confidence in himself and of hypocrisy" (*Ibid.*).

Lord said—not that He had actually rejected the Bishop, but that He felt such disgust at his tepidity—that in case of a fall into mortal sin the unworthy prelate should forfeit the friendship of God, and be utterly abandoned.

Was not, then, the threat in question called for by the circumstances of the case, especially when the offender was a bishop, who, as Bergier remarks, not only ought to be exempt from flagrant vice, but should be a conspicuous example of such virtues as these—ardent charity, indefatigable zeal, and indomitable courage?

The tepidity, however, herein before described, bears no resemblance to the state of that feeble soul which, though feeling no courage or no inclination to discharge its duties, does nevertheless discharge them; which is ever tormented by the idea that it must sink under the weight of its obligations, but still bears up, and which feels a natural inclination to grow cold, but offers a vigorous resistance. The forgetfulness of special duties cannot be compared with the omission of mere practices of piety; nor a neglect which works injury to the Church, with a languor of spirit which does no outward harm; nor culpable inaction or laziness in an unimportant office, with the shortcomings of weakness in an obscure and private station. Surely there is no kind of similarity between these two kinds of tepidity. So far Bergier.[12]

Let us, then, admire the goodness of God, Who, as St. Ambrose says, does not visit us on a sudden with the chastisements due to our offences, but first thunders in our ears, before His bolt is sped.[13] For thus precisely did He act in respect of this lukewarm Bishop. He gave him a gracious warning of the dangers which

---

[12] *De Miser. Div.* pp. 273, 274.

[13] "He does not vomit forth the unjust before first threatening them, in the hope that by His warning being converted they may escape their doom" (Serm. ii. *In Psalm.* cxviii.).

encompassed him, and pointed out the means of safety. "I counsel thee," said our Lord, "to buy of Me the gold of charity, purified from vanity and hypocrisy—a charity not lukewarm, but burning hot, which shall make thee rich indeed; I counsel thee to clothe thyself in the pure and white garment of a chaste and stainless life. Finally, I entreat thee to anoint thy eyes with the ointment of consideration, meditating upon thy last end —the most perfect cure for mental blindness." [14]

Such language as this is far from conveying the threat of a God desirous to cast off His creatures on account of negligence shown in His service. "This God of boundless love," says Bergier,[15] "though anxious that we should serve Him with the ardour of angels, yet in His infinite goodness adapts Himself to the weakness of our nature. He bears with us, and constantly warns us of the consequence of continued negligence, not because He means to reject us, but solely out of a desire for our good. He exhorts us to fervour in order that we may advance in virtue, and thereby not only secure our salvation, but lay up for ourselves an augmented stock of glory and of merit through all eternity." And if the substance of what our Lord spoke to this lukewarm Bishop amounted to an assurance that administered correction and urged him to repentance and fervour, solely from motives of love, and if, moreover, He supported this assurance by placing vividly before the Bishop's eyes the eternal reward awaiting his obedience, how little cause must we have for being cast down or losing heart in the service of God?

[14] "I counsel thee to buy of me gold fire-tried, that thou mayest be made rich, and mayest be clothed in white garments, and that the shame of thy nakedness may not appear, and anoint thy eyes with eye-salve that thou mayest see" (Apoc. iii. 18).

[15] "Without doubt God deserves to be served with all the fervour of angels, but out of goodness He is content to be served with the feebleness of humanity" (*Tabl. de la Miser. Div.* p. 274).

Let us rather trust implicitly in God; for spiritual faint-heartedness has its chief source, as Bergier observes,[16] in want of confidence in God, and in the idea of severity, which we falsely ascribe to Him. Let us hope in God, and we shall then love Him with more ardour and no longer find anything too hard that love requires at our hands. If our lowly condition puts but little in our power, let us do that little well, and God will prize it as highly as, according to the Gospel narrative, He valued the widow's mite bestowed in alms.[17] God will have regard, not to the importance of the service, but to the cheerfulness with which it is rendered.

CHAPTER VI.

On relapse into sin.

FIRST DIFFICULTY.—How can the unhappy sinner, after he has relapsed into sin, ever hope again to rise, again to return to God, and again to obtain pardon? For if it required a great exertion of God's mercy, nay, of His very omnipotence, to draw the sinner out of sin after a first fall, surely it must be a work of far greater difficulty after a second. Knowing as we do that the infirm man, who had endured paralysis for a continuous course of thirty-eight years, was threatened by Christ with a far worse fate if he fell again, how terrible must be the punishment awaiting the wretch who relapses into

---

[16] *Tabl. de la Miser. Div.* pp. 275, 276.   [17] St. Luke xxi. 3.

sin.[1] Has not Jesus Christ Himself told us in one of His parables, that after a relapse the devil would return and once more take possession of the soul from which he had been expelled; and not only so, but that he would bring with him seven other devils worse than himself, and bind that soul with chains stronger than before.[2]

Answer.—In a literal sense this parable was applied by the holy Fathers[3] to the case of the Jews, from whom, by the power of the future Messias, and through the medium of the Old Law the devil had been expelled, but into whom he had again entered in consequence of their rejection of the law of grace preached to them by Jesus Christ. Therefore, He had predicted that as a consequence of their monstrous ingratitude still worse evils should befall them in the ruin of the city of Jerusalem and of the Temple; so that they should be left for ever afterwards without prophet, without temple, and without sacrifice.

Further, in its mystic sense this parable was applied by the holy Fathers to the persons relapsed into sin. And from the point of view thus presented, it is certainly made perfectly manifest, that so far as mortal sins are concerned, we ought to spare no pains to avoid them. For what greater insult can we offer to God than to expel Him from the soul and introduce the devil in His place, thus declaring by our act that, having served under both masters, we prefer the service of the devil to that of God, thus putting the climax to our ingratitude? It is also made equally plain from this point of view that we

[1] "Behold thou art made whole, sin no more lest some worse thing happen to thee' St. John v. 14).

[2] "He taketh with him seven other spirits more wicked than himself, . . . and the last state of that man is worse than the first" (St. Matt. xii. 45 ; St. Luke xi. 26).

[3] See Cornelius à Lapide on this passage.

should avoid such sins, lest we acquire a habit of committing them, whereby the obstacles to amendment are enormously increased.

Although we ought for these reasons to use our most strenuous exertions to avoid relapsing into sin, still if we have the misfortune to find ourselves in the unhappy position of having so relapsed, we must bear in mind that what is difficult to us, is not so to God, to Whom all things are possible.[4] It is all the more incumbent on us to act thus, as God has promised to grant us grace in proportion to our need, so that "where sin abounded, grace might still more abound."[5] By grace the sinner who turns to God not only for pardon, but for the strength necessary for future amendment, shall without doubt find deliverance.

Surely if our Lord were averse to pardoning sinners a second time after a relapse, He would not have commanded St. Peter to forgive injuries repeated seventy times seven times, or, as the Council of Trent[6] interprets these words, every time they with due repentance make confession of their guilt. Let no one object that the keys were given by Christ to St. Peter also for the purpose of retaining sins, in other words, of closing the gates of Heaven against sinners. The keys were given by Christ to Peter, to enable him to open Heaven to the well-disposed among sinners; and if they be not used to open the gates to the ill-disposed, it is not the keys but their own obstinacy which keeps Heaven's gates closed against them, and prevents the keys from being used in their behalf.

---

[4] "No word shall be impossible with God" (St. Luke i. 37).

[5] Rom. v. 20.

[6] "That the sins they have confessed may be remitted by the priest, not once, but as often as they approach the tribunal in a penitential spirit" (Sess. xiv. capp. ii. iii.).

So far as to mortal sins. And next as to venial sins: it is quite clear that we should also exert ourselves to the utmost to avoid committing such sins with deliberation, and still more to avoid suffering the heart to grow attached to them, or ourselves to remain in them for any time; and to this end we should, on becoming conscious that we have fallen, at once ask pardon from God and resolve on amendment for the future; but when such sins are not the result of full deliberation, why, we have the authority of St. James for saying that we shall commit faults of this sort very frequently,[7] nor (with the exception of the Blessed Virgin and a few others especially privileged by God) have the saints themselves been exempt from the like failings. If we follow then the course indicated, no very fatal consequences are to be apprehended from venial sins.[8]

SECOND DIFFICULTY.—Is it not more correct to say, that God's promise to the sinner of pardon as often as he repents and resolves on a change of life, is a mere delusion? For what is it but a mockery of the sinner, on the one hand to urge, exhort, and press him, nay, even to impose on him the obligation to be converted and amend his life, and on the other to declare, that for him repentance is impossible? Here are the very words of Scripture: "It is impossible for those, who were once illuminated, have tasted also the heavenly gift, and were made partakers of the Holy Ghost, and are fallen away, to be renewed again to penance."[9] Who can hope for

[7] "For in many things we all offend" (St. James iii. 2).

[8] See *Introduction to the Devout Life* of St. Francis of Sales, ch. xx. p. 1.

[9] "For it is impossible for those who were once illuminated, have tasted also the heavenly gift and were made partakers of the Holy Ghost, . . . and are fallen away, to be renewed again to penance" (Heb. vi. 4, 6).

salvation in face of such a declaration? For there is not one of us but either has already too often relapsed into sin, or is liable to do so at any moment; and in either case, as we are here told, all repentance, and therefore all forgiveness, are impossibilities.

Answer.—Far from us be such fatal and false ideas of the Divine promises and of God Himself! Cornelius à Lapide asserts—and his assertion is fully borne out by St. John Chrysostom, Theodoretus, Theophylactus, Ecumenius, Acnion, Sedulius, Primasius, St. Ambrose, St. Jerome, St. Augustine, and others—that, in the opinion of almost all the early Fathers, the Apostle intended by the passage in question to condemn a current belief that the effects of Baptism could be repeated after a relapse on the part of the person who had once received that sacrament. For the Hebrews having before their conversion been accustomed to repeat the legal ceremony corresponding to Baptism, imagined after they became Christians that they could repeat the Christian ceremony with the same efficacy as on the first occasion.

In their explanation of this passage, Duhamel and Mgr. Martini take it in this sense, and agree with Cornelius à Lapide that the *illuminated* mentioned therein refers to those who had received Christian Baptism, as may be gathered from Origen,[10] from the Syriac version of the Bible, and from the earliest Fathers and Gentile theologians. On this ground Mgr. Martini, who agrees herein with St. Augustine, points out that the Apostle does not declare repentance to be impossible after a relapse into sin after Baptism, but that the renovation which was effected by Baptism, and whereby sin and its punishment had been remitted, cannot be

[10] Lib. ii. cap. i.

accomplished by the same means a second time, inasmuch as the sacrament cannot be conferred more than once.

And although some of our modern commentators interpret this passage as referring to the Sacrament of Penance, and consider the word *impossible* to mean *very difficult*, still even in this sense, Cornelius à Lapide, Tirinus, and Menochius, insist that the great difficulty must not be taken to apply to all sinners in general, but only to those who have been conspicuous for their ingratitude, such as apostates and obstinate heresiarchs, among whom, with the solitary exception of Berengarius, we know not of a single instance of a second conversion.

The passage might also, in one sense, be understood as referring to the Sacrament of Penance. For though strictly speaking it is not impossible, yet it is extremely difficulty, to approach that sacrament in a frame of mind so intensely contrite and otherwise well disposed as to ensure the remission, not only of guilt and its eternal punishment, but also of the temporal chastisements which are its due; and so fit the cleansed and beautified soul, if then set free from the body, for passing straight to Heaven, *as she would undoubtedly do* after Baptism.

It remains to be added, that their false interpretation of the text in question, herein combated, in the time of St. Cyprian gave rise to the heresy of Novatus and the Novatians, who taught that those who, after receiving the Sacrament of Baptism, relapsed into sin, ought no longer to be admitted to the Sacrament of Penance, or to pardon.

In like manner Tertullian also erroneously taught that such as fell into the sin of impurity should not be admitted more than once to the Sacrament of Penance.

All these errors, however, have been in far off ages condemned by the Church; for God has promised to forget all the sins of the sinner if he be contrite of heart and be converted, and at the earliest opportunity ready to disclose them in confession.[11]

THIRD DIFFICULTY.—But does not God compare sinners who have relapsed into sin after having been pardoned, or who have proved ungrateful for benefits received, to "the earth that drinketh in the rain which cometh often upon it . . . but which bringeth forth thorns and briers, is reprobate, and very near unto a curse whose end is to be burnt?"[12] Now if we are all, as we must acknowledge ourselves to be, ungrateful to God for His benefits, and either have relapsed into sin in time past, or are under a just apprehension of doing so in the future, how is it possible not to fear that we also may be rejected and fall under God's curse and have our final lot in Hell-fire?

Answer.—Cornelius à Lapide holds that in this passage the Apostle in so many words confirms his previous assertion, to the effect that the sin of apostasy, committed after the reception of very many of God's lights, graces, and favours, is most grievous; that the apostate is very nigh unto a curse; and that, if he repent not, he shall hear the thunder of the malediction which consigns him to eternal fire.

Be it further remarked, that here the question relates not to ground merely barren, which yields but a scant

---

[11] "If the wicked do penance . . . I will not remember all the iniquities that he hath done" (Ezech. xviii. 21). "I say not to thee till seven times; but till seventy times seven times" (St. Matt. xviii. 22). "That by the sentence of the priest the penitent may be absolved from his sins, not once, but as often as he has recourse to his tribunal" (Council of Trent, Sess. xiv. cap. 2).

[12] Heb. vi. 7, 8.

return to all the outlay and labour expended by the husbandmen in endeavouring to render it productive,—type of the man who neglects to act up to all the inspirations of God—but that the question relates to a soil of so bad and unkindly a nature, that though often watered by the fertilizing dews of Heaven, it not only brings forth no good fruit, but produces a plentiful crop of thorns and thistles, the rooting out of which adds greatly to the labour of the cultivator. Such a soil is the type of those sinners who refuse to correspond with the call to repentance and with the means of salvation offered them by God; but who, instead of the fruit of good works, ungratefully bring forth nothing but the briers and sharp thorns of sin. Such sinners as these, so long as they live in this miserable state, being most deservedly detested by God, *are reprobate.* Nevertheless, even when reduced to this condition, they are not called absolutely cursed, but only "very near to a curse," in other words, conditionally cursed; whereby it is signified that if they amend not, they shall be surprised by death when it is least expected, and undergo the curse of condemnation to eternal fire.[13]

FOURTH DIFFICULTY.—But seeing that the Apostle very plainly lays down, "that if we sin wilfully after having the knowledge of the truth, there is now left no sacrifice for sins,"[14] how can we hope for pardon after our numerous relapses?

Answer.—Cornelius à Lapide, Tirinus, and Menochius, affirm that in this passage the Apostle refers solely to the sin of apostasy, which they averred to be, beyond

---

[13] "Depart from me, you cursed, into everlasting fire" (St. Matt. xxv. 41).
[14] Heb. x. 26.

a doubt, most difficult of remission.[15] Nevertheless (as Cornelius à Lapide himself observes in another place), to deny even to apostates the benefit of repentance, when from their heart they detest their sin, is so far from being in accord with the doctrine of the Church, that it is a revival of the error of the Novatians, long ago, as we remarked towards the close of the second difficulty, actually proscribed by the Church.

Cornelius à Lapide and Tirinus add that, strictly speaking, there remained, in the proper sense of the term, no victim of propitiation nor hope of pardon for those unrepentant Hebrews who had apostatized from Jesus Christ and relapsed into Judaism. As long as they continued in their apostasy they could derive no saving benefit from Jesus Christ Whom they denied, nor from that expected Messias, Who was never to come; and none from the sacrifices of the Old Law, which had been abrogated and made of no effect; so that whilst they persevered in this apostate state there was for them neither sacrifice nor pardon, but only the terrible prospect of God's avenging justice.

Duhamel also reads this passage as applying especially to those Hebrews who had apostatized from Jesus Christ, and says that, having by their apostasy shown their contempt for the Sacrifice on the Cross, they had no other expiatory sacrifice to fall back on.

A similar explanation is offered by Bergier,[16] who says that there remained for them no other propitiatory victim after they had despised and trampled on Jesus Christ, the only One capable of cancelling their sins. "It is indeed," he writes, "a truly terrible thing to fall whilst in this state into the hands of that God Whom they

---

[15] "With difficulty and scarcely is a sacrifice left for sin by which it may be expiated."

[16] *Tabl. de la Miser. Div.* p. 261.

have despised and trampled on." Such woeful consequences, however, do not attend all relapses into sin.

FIFTH DIFFICULTY.—When one reflects that "no man putting his hand to the plough," that is to say, who enters on the service of God, "and looking back," that is to say, who halts or swerves from that service, "is fit for the kingdom of Heaven,"[17] how can any of us presume to think that the picture here painted does not represent his own case? If so, how can we ever be at peace, whilst we are haunted by so well grounded a dread of our being unfit to enter the kingdom of Heaven?

Answer.—The Evangelist is in this passage speaking of one who, being called to the Apostleship by Jesus Christ, asked to be allowed, before following the Lord, to return to his home and take leave of its inmates. It was on this occasion that Jesus Christ, in order to teach His ministers how necessary to the success of their labours was detachment from all worldly cares and solicitude, held up for their warning the picture of the ploughman who, averting his eyes from the plough, is no longer able properly to go on with his work. Duhamel says that our Lord wished thereby to teach us, that to be an efficient minister of the Gospel, a man should not have his mind distracted by cares foreign to his sacred ministry. So also say Menochius and Tirinus, who couple this text with the following from St. Paul: "No man being a soldier to God entangleth himself with secular businesses."[18] Thus these commentators consider both texts to relate to the same subject-matter.

---

[17] St. Luke ix. 62.   [18] 1 Cor. ix. 24; 2 Tim. ii. 4.

CHAPTER VII.

On the number of the Chosen.

FIRST DIFFICULTY.—Sinners, however greatly they may desire their own conversion, cannot derive from the Catholic religion any assured hope of salvation. Would it not, in point of fact, argue on their part the most presumptuous audacity to hope, after the commission of countless sins, to be among the select few, seeing that many theologians, taking their stand upon texts of Scripture and the opinion of the Fathers,[1] lay it down as an article of faith that very few shall be saved? Surely this is made quite clear by the repetition of the text in St. Matthew, "Many are called but few are chosen."[2]

Answer.—I must, in the first place, preface my explanation of the meaning of this text by the observation—made also by Bergier—that among Catholic commentators, all cited by the author just named, there is so great a diversity of opinion upon the question whether the number of the saved shall be few or many, and that so great is the divergence of view among the holy Fathers themselves, that the mere enunciation of their opinions would more than fill a reasonably sized volume. On none of these opinions of the Catholic commentators has the faculty of theology ever pronounced any censure; whilst Holy Church has specially condemned Father Berruyer for having affirmed that the word "chosen"

[1] Bergier's treatise *On the True Religion*, vol. xii. p. 202. Edit. Paris, 1784; *Diction. Histor.* title Elec.
[2] St. Matt. xx. 16; xxii. 14.

meant the faithful who are saved, to the exclusion of every other meaning. In this state of the case, says Bergier, what article of faith can be made to rest on a text susceptible of so many meanings?³ Moreover Holy Church herself, who is the sole authority on disputed matters, has never given any decision on the question involved in the present controversy, and confines herself to affirming, that to God alone belongs the knowledge of the number that shall be saved.

If indeed there be a consensus among the holy Fathers upon any point, it is on the meaning of the day's wages paid, according to the parable, to the labourers in the vineyard. All the Fathers, as Cornelius à Lapide remarks, with the exception of St. Basil (who, according to Maldonatus's commentary on the twentieth chapter of St. Matthew, refers these words to a temporal reward) are agreed that the day's wages said to have been given to the labourers, must be understood to mean eternal life. "Therefore," continues Cornelius à Lapide (in his commentary, section *juxta hunc sensum*, on this same chapter of St. Matthew), "many hold that the words of our Lord in this parable relate exclusively to the elect, and have no reference whatsoever to the reprobate." In support of this statement he cites St. Jerome, St. Augustine, St. Gregory Nanzianzen, St. Anselm, Tertullian, St. Thomas, Maldonatus, Suarez, and Valentia, to whom may be added the Venerable Cardinal Bellarmine.⁴ Salmeron, Paolo da Palacio of Grenada, and Cornelius à Lapide, consider the opinion thus vouched for by authorities to be extremely probable, as it affords a complete solution to the question why it was that all the labourers received the same hire.

³ "God, Who alone knows the number of the elect that shall be received into the happy mansions of Heaven" (Dom. 1 Quadr.).
⁴ See his works, vol. ii. l. v. p. 205, *On a Happy Eternity*.

Solution of Difficulties.

In the second place, Salmeron (in the seventh volume of his treatises),[5] and Cornelius à Lapide (towards the close of his nineteenth chapter), both make an observation that is most apposite. They say that the whole scope of the parable in question is to be gathered from the chapter which precedes it; for it is spoken merely in elucidation of the verse: "Many that are first shall be last, and the last shall be first," with which words the nineteenth chapter concludes. That this view is correct may be inferred from the use of the conjunction "for," found in the Greek version and in some corrected Latin codices at the opening of the twentieth chapter, which accordingly in these copies begins thus: "For the kingdom of Heaven is like," &c. A similar inference follows from the use of the word "so," at the end of chapter nineteen, and in verse sixteen of chapter twenty, in juxtaposition with the same words in both places.

In point of fact the Bible narrative runs thus: A young man having asked the Lord "What good shall I do to have life everlasting?" Jesus answered and said: "If thou wilt enter into life, keep the commandments," and added afterwards, "If thou wilt be perfect, go sell what thou hast and give to the poor and come and follow Me." Whereupon the young man "went away sad, for he had great possessions."[6]

St. Peter, who was present, thereupon took occasion thus to question his Divine Master:[7] "Behold we have left all things and have followed Thee what then shall we have." And Jesus answered: "You who have followed Me shall sit with Me on twelve seats judging the twelve tribes of Israel. And every one who hath left" family "or lands for My name's sake shall receive an hundred-

---

[5] N. 33, p. 210.   [6] St. Matt. xix. 17, 21, 22.
[7] St. Matt. xix. 27.

fold and life everlasting." Our Lord then suddenly concludes by saying: "So, many that are first shall be last, and the last shall be first."[8] Now, as in this magnificent promise Jesus had given the Apostles precedence in dignity over the Patriarchs—the judge being superior to the judged—and as further He had given them precedence in merit over the young man who had scrupulously from his youth upwards kept the commandments—which the Apostles, or at least some of them, might not have done—this abrupt conclusion might have appeared somewhat obscure. In order, therefore, to make His meaning quite clear to His disciples, Jesus at once proceeded to elucidate it by the parable of the labourers in the vineyard. This parable represents these labourers as hired by a certain householder and sent to work in his vineyard, some at the first, others at the third, and others at the sixth and ninth hours of the day respectively; then at the eleventh hour others were hired and sent to work. And when evening came the Lord of the vineyard directed his steward to call the labourers and pay them their hire, beginning from the last hired, and so on up in order to the first, giving them all from last to first the same hire. Our Lord concludes the parable with the identical words with which he closes the nineteenth chapter, namely, "so shall the last be first and the first last;" adding, "for many are called but few are chosen."[9]

This being premised you will the better understand the illustrious Suarez when he says, that it is in direct contravention of the concurrent opinion of the Fathers

---

[8] St. Matt. xix. 28—30.

[9] "Call the labourers and pay them their hire, beginning from the last even to the first. And they also received every man a penny. So shall the last be first, and the first last. For many are called but few chosen" (St. Matt. xx. 8, 10, 16).

to infer from this parable that but few shall be saved, and that it would be doing the greatest violence to the context to interpret its closing sentence as referring to the reprobate as well as to the just. How indeed, he asks, could the Lord of the vineyard possibly cause the labourers to be called together with a direction that each should receive the amount of his daily hire—by which all the Fathers understand eternal life—if they had not all earned it? And how could that Lord of the vineyard have thus answered the labourers who murmured, "I will also give to this last even as to thee,"[10] if he had not given a common recompense to all? Hence, we see, continues Suarez—and Salmeron uses the same language—that many who were last to get a call, shall be first to receive a reward, and *vice versâ*.

Salmeron contends that this interpretation fits in best with the literal sense of the parable, and Suarez, that it is the simplest and most obvious one, both as regards the meaning of the words used, and the support it receives from the whole narrative in the parable itself, wherein one band of labourers is called first and then the others in succession; while the reward is afterwards distributed by the steward to each in the reverse order of his calling by the direct command of the Lord of the vineyard.

Moreover, when we see that the postponement of payment to the first called was not made with the view of wholly depriving him of his stipulated hire, we become altogether unable to reconcile our minds to the notion that any of those can be reprobate who have received a reward, which all the Fathers agree in interpreting to mean eternal life. That the Fathers so interpret it appears from St. Jerome,[11] from St. Augustine,[12] and

---

[10] St. Matt. xx. 14. [11] Bk. ii. against Jovinus and on St. Matt.
[12] Hom. lix. on the Word of the Lord.

from St. Chrysostom, and St. Anselm, and St. Gregory Nazianzen,[13] from St. Gregory the Great,[14] and Tertullian.[15]

Of this opinion is Salmeron.[16] He says the whole scope of the parable is a comparison between the ministers of the New and the Old Law, wherein the former are preferred. Maldonatus gives it as his opinion that the scope of the parable is to show that the reward of eternity is not dependent on the duration of the work done, because one man may do as much in an hour as another in a day.[17] Hence it follows that no one should pride himself on his call being of an old date, "for many who are last shall be first, and first, last."

Cornelius à Lapide, in his commentary on St. Matthew, says the parable is to be understood as meaning that many are called to ordinary grace and the observance of the Divine commandments, but few are chosen for a vocation to the sublime degree of grace and the observance of the evangelical counsels; and he cites a variety of authorities in support of this position. This reading appears to be most in accord with its literal interpretation, having regard to the occasion which called forth the parable, namely, the conduct of the young man, who, when called to the observance of the evangelical counsels "went away sad," in other words, failed to correspond with his vocation.[19]

[13] Orat. xl. On Holy Baptism.
[14] Vol. ii. bk. ii. Hom. xvi. on Ezechiel.
[15] Book on Monogam.
[16] Vol. vii. tract. 33, sect. The scope then, &c.
[17] "Being made perfect in a short space, he fulfilled a long time" (Wisdom iv. 13).
[18] Chap. xx. 16, sect. *Denique nonnulli.*
[19] In order to be more thoroughly convinced that the parable taken literally has no semblance whatsoever of being in any way connected with the reprobate, it is only necessary to mark how all its language, in its most obvious sense, tallies with the explanations above offered. In the first place, observe that, an agreement for

Let us next advert to the fourteenth verse of the twenty-second chapter of St. Matthew, wherein our Lord concludes the parable of the marriage feast by the same

payment of specific wages was made with the band of labourers first hired, a general promise only was given to those hired at the third, sixth, and ninth hours, and not one word of promise to those last sent. "And having agreed with the labourers for a penny a day. . . . I will give you what shall be just. . . . Go ye also into my vineyard" (St. Matt. xx. 2, 4, 7). According to Salmeron, the first class of labourers represent generally the ancient Fathers who lived under the law of nature, and also imperfect Christians; the second class typifies proficients in virtue; and the last is meant to stand for those who are perfect. Or the first class may be taken to represent the Old Testament Fathers and those imperfect Christians who serve God chiefly from a hope of future reward; and the last to represent perfect Christians, apostolic ministers and religious, who serve God from pure love, abstractively from the hope of reward. In the second place observe, that the first called were the last to be paid their hire, and, *vice versâ*, the last called were the first to receive it. Now if the Fathers who lived under the Old Dispensation are the class designated as the first called to work out their salvation, "Most surely," says the Venerable Cardinal Bellarmine—agreeing herein with Salmeron and others—"Christians, though the last called, are more quickly paid." Adam, Noe, and all the patriarchs and prophets, had not only to labour for a protracted term during life, but to wait hundreds, nay, thousands of years in Limbo after death for their reward; whilst, on the other hand, the Apostles and martyrs laboured but for a brief space and at once at death received their reward; or, as Salmeron and St. Irenæus (towards the close of his work against heretics, bk. iv. p. 24) teach, they were rewarded, so far as the Apostles were concerned, even during life, by the sight of and conversation with Jesus Christ, Who, being God, is the object of beatitude; for which reason He said to His disciples, "Blessed are the eyes that see the things which you see" (St. Luke x. 23). Again, if we understand the passage to refer to imperfect and perfect Christians, we all know the difficulty experienced by persons attached to the world in working out their salvation, and how, by reason of their numerous short-comings, they will have to undergo a long detention in Purgatory before attaining their reward. Whereas the perfect, and especially those who observe the evangelical counsels, serve the Lord with cheerfulness and freedom from anxiety, and after death,

words, "For many are called but few are chosen." Here, says Bergier, the meaning of these words will be more easily gathered if we refer to the two parables having but few faults to atone for, will receive a speedy and more abundant reward. In the third place, observe that, when at the end of the day those who had worked longest coming forward to be paid, found to their disappointment that they received no more than the others, they murmured against the master of the house. "But when the first also came, they thought that they should receive more, and they also received every man a penny, and receiving it they murmured, saying, these last have worked but one hour" (St. Matt. xx. 10—12). Here we have the thoughts and language of the imperfect, whether those who lived under the old, or who live under the Christian dispensation. As to those under the Old Law, they imagined, that because of their protracted life, and the greater difficulty of working out their salvation, arising from want of the sacramental aids, from less grace, and fewer incentives to virtue, the road to which had not yet been marked out by Christ's footsteps, they should be entitled to a larger measure of reward than those who lived under the New Law, and who were favoured by such abundant means and graces in the way of salvation. A similar observation applies to imperfect Christians. They, in consequence of their attachment to worldly goods, find more difficulty in observing the commandments than the perfect do in the observance of the evangelical counsels; and hence they infer from the greater obstacles they have to overcome in doing good, that they shall receive an ampler reward for the doing of it. Both the one and the other find occasion to murmur. The Jews murmured when they found the Christians, who were called to the faith, preferred before them by reason of their own stubbornness. And Christians are found to murmur when imperfect and worldly in their notions, and guiding their judgments not by the light of faith, they rail against Religious Orders and ministers of the Gospel, declaring them to be a burthen on society, and not only not equal to, but inferior to themselves in merit. But our Lord will make it manifest to them: "Friend, I do thee no wrong" (St. Matt. xx. 13), that He does them no wrong when He gives a preference to those whom they undervalue; for He prizes good actions in proportion to the greater charity, grace, and purity of intention which accompany them. In the fourth place, observe that the master of the house pronounces the *eye* of the labourers who murmured, in other words, their process of thought and reasoning, to be evil, but only in a lesser degree, as generally happens with the imperfect. Moreover, He speaks not

contained in the twenty-first chapter immediately preceding; for it is abundantly clear from the occurrence of the conjunction "and" at the opening of the twenty-

positively but interrogatively, and seems to ask, will you cast an evil eye upon an act of kindness ("Is thy eye evil because I am good?" St. Matt. xx. 15) which I wish to show to these labourers who were the last to be hired, when at the same time I am not doing any wrong to you, who have received your stipulated pay? Or to use the words of Job x., "Hast thou ears of flesh," where we must supply the silently understood completion of the sentence, "far be it from thee that thou shouldest be so." In the fifth place, observe that all the labourers are said to receive an equal amount of money. "Thou hast made them equal to us" (St. Matt. xx. 12). This equality relates to the substance only of beatitude, consisting of the beatific vision, and in the parable, typified by the daily hire given to all alike; but the beatific essence will be apportioned to each one in quantity according to his merits, as is declared by St. Gregory the Great (vol. ii. bk. ii. Hom. xvi. in Ezech, p. 83), Salmeron and Bellarmine (Opusc. vol. ii. bk. v. p 205). In this particular, therefore, the parable is in accord with the sayings of our Lord: "That in Heaven there are many mansions, and that one man shall be appointed ruler over ten, and another over five cities; and thus we have a full explanation of how the diversity of merits, rewarded by a corresponding diversity in the degrees of glory, is reconciled with the payment at the same time to all alike of the same hire, that is to say, of eternal beatitude. St. Gregory Nazianzen assigns various reasons for the equality in the hire given to the labourers who were last employed, with that given to the first. He says it was (1) because the former would have at once obeyed the call, had it been made earlier. (2) They left the amount of their hire to the goodness of the master of the vineyard, whereas the others, as we saw, bargained for theirs. (3) Because the master of the vineyard perceived their readiness to accept gratefully whatever he chose to give, whereas he foresaw the discontent of the others (Orat. xl. on Holy Bapt. p. 861, D. Edit. Paris, 1583). Finally, observe that the Divine Redeemer closes the parable with the words, "so that," or, as Salmeron paraphrases the passage, "for these reasons, and in the manner aforesaid, I will, out of My bounty and liberality, bestow a greater recompense on those called last, although they endured less labour and served a briefer time, than on those who endured more, and served longer; because the former served Me with greater grace, greater fervour of charity, and greater purity of intention than the latter."

second chapter, "*And* Jesus answering," &c., that it is a continuation of the twenty-first.

Now, the parable of the two sons told by their father to go to work in his vineyard,[20] that of the servants and the son and heir killed by the husbandmen,[21] and lastly that of the wedding feast,[22] all these parables, but more especially the last, which is repeated with little variation in St. Luke,[23] under the title of the great supper, show with wonderful clearness, that the epithet first-called is used to designate the Hebrews,[24] to whom indeed, as Mgr. Martini points out, and as is apparent from the Gospel itself, our Lord's discourse was principally addressed.[25] For all the Jews, with the exception of some few, scattered among unbelieving nations, were called to the faith through the preaching and miracles of Jesus Christ and His Apostles, " Many were called:" few were converted ; "few were chosen."

Salmeron and Martini[26] give a similar explanation of this parable in their exposition of it; and Calino[27] makes the further observations, that in place of the invited guests who refused to attend, and who represent the Hebrews, the marriage tables were filled with a motley crowd composed of the poor, the lame, and the maimed —an apt figure of the Gentiles ; and that of all the guests who attended the feast, one alone—and that because he was not clad in the wedding garment, which was essential —was cast into exterior darkness.[28] Would it not there-

[20] St. Matt. xxi. 28.
[21] St. Matt. xxi. 33.
[22] St. Matt. xxii. 2.
[23] St. Luke xiv. 16.
[24] "And they knew that He spoke of them" (St. Matt. xxi. 45).
[25] "Because no man hath hired us" (St. Matt. xx. 7).
[26] Turin. Edit. 1771.
[27] Lecture xxi. vol. iv. bk. i.
[28] St. Matt. xxii. 13.

fore be a contradiction of the whole tenor of the parable itself to hold that the concluding words, "few are chosen," mean that few are saved?

If, indeed, any lesson (without going so far as to ask for proofs) is to be derived from the parable, it is, as Calino and Bergier remark, that we may safely infer that but few are damned and many are saved.

Thus five of the ten virgins went in unto the marriage, and the door was shut against as many more.[29] Of the three servants who were intrusted with their Lord's money, two received a recompense, and one alone was punished.[30] Our Lord compares the good seed to the children of the kingdom, and the cockle to the children of the wicked one.[31] Now, as in every well-cultivated field—and surely the Church may be so called—the good grain is not only not less than, but is greatly in excess of the cockle, so among Christians, at least, the saved must be much more numerous than the lost; and although, as St. Augustine remarks,[32] the straw, which is the symbol of the wicked, is more bulky than the grain in the barn, which symbolizes the Church; yet if we regard, as we ought to do, not the aggregate bulk, but the number of the individual straws, and compare it with the number of the grains of wheat, we shall undoubtedly find for every straw as many grains of wheat as were once in the ear attached to the stalk.

Moreover, He likens the just to sheep, and the wicked to goats.[33] Now we know from every day's experience that the former are far more numerous than the latter, whose numbers are purposely kept down, in consequence of the damage done by them in browsing on shrubs and trees.

---

[29] Cap. xxv. [30] *Ibid.* [31] St. Matt. xiii. 38.
[32] *Cont. Cuscon.* lib. iii. cap. lxvi. [33] St. Matt. xxv. 32, 33.

In like manner He likens the just to the good fish, and the wicked to the bad fish;[34] and certainly the case was never known of a net which contained more bad fish to be cast out than good fish to be gathered in.

Lastly, bear in mind that our Lord bids the reapers first to gather the cockle into small heaps to burn it, and says that the angels of Heaven shall come and separate the wicked from the midst of the just.[35]

Now, in making the separation between materials that are mixed together, it is in accordance with order and with usage to pick out the less numerous ingredients from the more numerous; and we see that in many places of Scripture this course of proceeding, and not the reverse, is supposed to be followed.[36] Wherefore St. Augustine, alluding to the parable of the wheat and tares, bids some who had wickedly deserted from the standard of the Cross to control their transports, and not to allow themselves to be carried away by the sight of a few tares, thinly sown up and down through the rich expanse of corn that covered the earth.[37]

"Therefore," says Salmeron, "that closing sentence of the parable, 'Many are called but few are chosen,' ought not to terrify, but ought rather to console us; for both the many and the few receive the daily hire of eternal beatitude. Even if we have greatly sinned, we may well be animated to the utmost fervour in the

[34] St. Matt, xiii. 47, seq.
[35] St. Matt. xiii. 30, 49.
[36] Exodus xxix. 27; Lev. xx. 24—26; Deut. iv. 41; Numb. xxii. 26; Josue i. 14; Judith ii. 7; 1 Esdras x. 11; 2 Esdras xiii. 3.
[37] "Let these impious deserters be restrained by the boundless fertility of the corn-fields, and let them not presume to pride themselves on the few tares they see scattered here and there" (*Contr. Cresc.* lib. iii. cap. lxvii. t. vii. Edit. Ven. 1750).

practice of virtue, for our reward will be proportionately great; and in us will be realized the saying of our Lord with respect to harlots and publicans,[38] as well as that of the Wise Man with respect to the fervent, 'Being made perfect in a short space, he fulfilled a long time.'"[39]

SECOND DIFFICULTY.—On the other hand, St. Paul says, "All run indeed, but one receiveth the prize."[40] Who then will presume to hope that he shall be the lucky winner?

Answer.—This text, if well considered, ought to encourage us to strive for one of the first prizes, as runners at the starting-post brace themselves for victory. Calino sums up the meaning of the text thus. He says[41] that although all mankind, Gentiles, Jews, unbelievers, heretics, and schismatics, engage in the race which is supposed to lead up to the goal of happiness, "all indeed run;" nevertheless, that none but those who keep to the one straight course of the true faith and the observance of the Divine commandments gain the reward—"but one receiveth the prize."

Tirinus explains how this passage was written by St. Paul with special reference to himself, as though he should say, "I have laboured with all my power to preach the Gospel to you, and looked for nothing in return; I made myself all things to all men, and spared not myself in the race—in other words, in the Apostolic ministry—for I strive for the prize which is the portion of the few."

---

[38] "The publicans and sinners shall go before you into the Kingdom of Heaven" (St. Matt. xxi. 31).
[39] Wisdom iv. 13.
[40] 1 Cor. ix. 24.
[41] "Gentiles, Hebrews, heretics, the reprobate, run in the race, but the chosen of the Christians alone receive the prize."

H

Cornelius à Lapide agrees in opinion with Tirinus, and both he and St. John Chrysostom add that St. Paul, in saying that one should receive the prize, did not mean to convey that no one else should receive it, for, as Cornelius à Lapide further observes, not to the first in the race alone is a prize awarded, but a prize is allotted also to the second, third, and fourth.

St. Paul alluded exclusively to "one," without mentioning a second, third, or fourth, in order to emphasize the fact that he aspired to win the prize by superior excellence, which it is not given to all the elect to achieve, but to the few alone who, not content with the observance of the Divine commandments, strive after perfection by practising the Evangelical Counsels also in the true spirit of heroes.

"It is a contemptible thing for a man to say," adds St. John Chrysostom, "'for me it is enough to be saved,' because it is the duty of every one to endeavour to take the first rank and carry off the first prize."[42]

Lastly, the same commentator, Tirinus, goes on to say that others explain the passage to mean that each one should run in such a manner as to ensure his own appropriate reward, and that this is the sum and substance of St. Paul's words.[43]

Taken, indeed, in a strictly literal sense, the text, "but one receiveth the prize," would lead to the conclusion that no one but the Blessed Virgin Mary had attained salvation—a conclusion obviously inadmissible. Therefore if we would not be driven into absurdities and contradictions, we are compelled to accept the foregoing or similar explanations.

---

[42] "So run that you may obtain" (1 Cor. ix. 24).

[43] "It is the part of a sluggish soul to say, Enough for me . . . if I be saved, . . . for each one ought to strive to carry off . . . the first prize" (St. Chrysostom).

Solution of Difficulties.

THIRD DIFFICULTY.—St. Peter says that, *although the earth was thickly peopled at the time of the deluge, only eight souls were saved in the ark.*[44] Is not this a proof of the small number that are saved?

Answer.—We are not to conclude, from the mere assertion that only eight souls were saved from the deluge, that all the rest who were buried in its waters were therefore damned; for St. Augustine says that St. Peter had here in view not eternal, but temporal life, and accordingly used the phrase, eight souls, to signify eight persons, as in ordinary conversation a town is said to contain so many souls, the meaning of which phrase is, so many inhabitants. The text, then, must be understood to mean that only eight persons were saved alive from the deluge, and that all others perished in its waters.

But the Scripture does not countenance the assertion that the countless hosts who found a watery grave were damned; nay, more, the above-named illustrious Doctor, in addition to St. Jerome and Rupert—as quoted by Cornelius à Lapide towards the close of his Commentary on the sixth chapter of Genesis—holds that many of them were saved by contrition. In this opinion Mgr. Martini, Cardinal Bellarmine,[45] and Calino[46] concur.

If, indeed, we reflect on the circumstances which attended this mighty retribution, we may fairly come to the conclusion that very many of them were saved. In the first place, they witnessed the verification of Noe's warnings, and the fulfilment of his prediction respecting

---

[44] "Which had been some time incredulous, when they waited for the patience of God in the days of Noe, when the ark was building, wherein a few, that is, eight, souls were saved by water" (1 St. Peter iii. 20).

[45] *De Anima Christ.* lib. iv. cap. xiii.

[46] *Lez. Sacre*, t. iv. ch. iv. n. 18.

the impending catastrophe. In the second place, they beheld beasts of every kind, moved by an impulse from Heaven, taking shelter in the ark; and lastly, because the gradual advance of the chastising element gave time for repentance and an appeal to God for pardon, according to the saying, "Vexation maketh one to understand,"[47] and God ordered all things with a view to their conversion.

Hence Tirinus says, that although as long as Noe was building the ark, men refused to believe in the reality of the punishment which he predicted was impending over them on account of their sins, and flattered themselves that God would be still forbearing and overlook their iniquities: nevertheless, after they saw the floodgates of Heaven open and the universal deluge begun, they believed, repented, and were converted. Therefore through drowning they were saved, and in common with others of the just were consigned to Limbo, whence they were all together finally liberated and transported to Heaven by Jesus Christ.

Cornelius à Lapide says that this is the true sense of the passage, and he very happily remarks, as does also Bellarmine, that although the souls of all the others had been liberated from Limbo by Christ, St. Peter[48] made mention only of these eight, lest his silence as to them should lead us to infer, as it easily might, that they had been eternally lost.

Duhamel is of opinion that numbers were converted by the preaching and exhortations of Noe, when the deluge was impending. This view is confirmed by what St. Peter writes in a subsequent verse, to the effect that

---

[47] "Vexation alone shall make you understand what you hear" (Isaias xxviii. 19).

[48] Cornelius à Lapide *In Epist.* 1 *Petri* iv. 13; Bellarm. *De Anima Christi*, lib. iv. cap. xiii.

if the death of Christ was efficacious to save the incredulous who were thus converted at the very last extremity of danger to life, how much more efficacious must be the saving waters of Baptism to make the first-fruits of the faithful partakers in the Resurrection. "Hence," concludes Duhamel, "it is by far the more probable opinion that the greater part of those who perished in the deluge were aroused from their incredulity and obstinacy when they saw death inevitable and pending, than that they died in their folly and stubborn pride.

FOURTH DIFFICULTY.—Since St. John says in the Apocalypse "that the stars" (meaning thereby the just) "fall to earth, as figs are cast to the ground when shaken by a mighty wind," what can poor sinners expect?

Answer.—Commentators explain this text as referring to the woeful period of Antichrist, when just men of the sublimest virtue, so-called stars of Heaven, shall under the scourge of persecution fall into error, as green figs fall from the tree before a tempest. Duhamel, who places the fall of the just here described during the last days of the world, holds this opinion.[49]

Tirinus quotes Ribera, Pereira, and Cornelius à Lapide, who are all of opinion that by stars here are meant comets, thunderbolts, balls of fire, and other burning meteors resembling stars of an unknown and prodigious magnitude, form, and motion, which God will cast down upon the earth to the consternation of men. Such, too, is the opinion of Mgr. Martini.

Referring to the words "as the fig tree casteth its green" (that is its unripe) "figs when it is shaken by a great wind,"[50] Cornelius à Lapide explains them to mean

[49] V. 16.

[50] "And the stars from Heaven fell upon the earth, as the fig-tree casteth its green figs when it is shaken by a great wind" (Apoc. vi. 13).

that God, provoked by the sins of men, will bring the world to an end sooner than they looked for, or than in the course of nature it would have come to pass.

It is quite apparent also from the context of this chapter of the Apocalypse, that it refers to the end of the world, and so it is understood by a vast majority of the holy Fathers, and authors cited by Tirinus. This interpretation is further confirmed by what Jesus Christ said in St. Matthew with reference to these days, namely, "that the charity of many would grown cold,"[51] and, as His words are narrated in St. Luke, "that faith shall scarcely be found upon earth."[52]

FIFTH DIFFICULTY.—If, as we read in Holy Writ, "of all the numerous inhabitants in the five cities of the plain, three persons only were saved from the conflagration,"[53] surely very few also shall be saved from eternal fire, seeing how iniquity abounds in the world.

Answer.—If the family of Lot alone were saved when Sodom was burned to the ground, remember that the inhabitants of the city of Segor, which was infected with the like crimes, were all spared, as we are told in Genesis [54] at Lot's intercession.

Instead of being dismayed at God's judgment upon Sodom, ought we not rather contemplate this His goodness and clemency, and dwell on His promises to pardon sin, and His aversion to punish the obstinacy of sinners.

---

[51] "The charity of many shall grow cold" (St. Matt. xxiv. 12).

[52] "But yet the Son of Man when He cometh shall He find, think you, faith on the earth?" (St. Luke xviii. 8).

[53] "And the Lord rained upon Sodom and Gomorrha [and according to Deut. xxix. 23, on Adama and Seboim] brimstone and fire from the Lord out of Heaven. . . . He delivered Lot out of the destruction of the cities" (Genesis xix. 24, 29).

[54] "Behold also in this I have heard thy prayer, not to destroy the city for which thou hast spoken" (Genesis xix. 21).

For we read that our Lord could not resist what at first sight appears the too importunate prayer of Abraham, who, on hearing from the angels that they were about to destroy Sodom, besought the Lord to spare the city if fifty just men were found within its walls, and who afterwards, gaining courage from concessions made to his repeated requests, went on lowering the number which was to suffice for the sparing of the city, until he obtained a promise that if only ten such men could be found there, the whole population should be saved.[55]

And as God was willing to spare all the inhabitants of Sodom if only ten just men were found within its walls, so also we read in Jeremias [56] that the Lord promised the prophet to spare all Jerusalem, which had been doomed to become the prey of the Chaldeans, if only one just man could be found therein. Nay, so anxious did the Lord show Himself to pardon, that He commanded the prophet to go about through the streets of Jerusalem and all its broad places to see, to consider diligently, and to seek if a single just man could be found there, so great was His desire to exercise the prerogative of pardon towards all.[57]

SIXTH DIFFICULTY.—Who can flatter himself that he shall be saved, when, as we read in Holy Writ, in punishment of the want of faith, out of over 600,000 of the children of Israel who quitted Egypt, two alone,

---

[55] "I will not destroy it for the sake of ten" (Genesis xviii. 32).
[56] Jerem. v. 1.
[57] "Go about through the streets of Jerusalem, and see, and consider, and seek in the broad places thereof, if you can find a man that executeth judgment and seeketh faith; and I will be merciful unto it:" that is to say, as Cornelius à Lapide notes from the Hebrew text, unto the entire city (Jerem. v. 1).

Josue and Caleb, entered the promised land which is the symbol of Heaven?[58]

Answer.—True it is, that of the over 600,000 of the children of Israel quitting Egypt, Josue and Caleb alone entered the promised land; but, on the other hand, it also appears from the book of Numbers[59] that 601,730 others who were under the command of Josue, without a single exception entered into that land.

Moreover, Cornelius à Lapide[60] observes that the 600,000 and upwards who were not permitted to enter, thereby had a temporal and not an eternal punishment inflicted on them, and that probably, like Moses and Aaron, they exchanged an eternal for a temporal evil.

Unless, indeed, it may not rather be inferred from the foregoing, as a learned writer suggests, that if salvation were difficult under the Old Law, of which Moses was the symbol, it is a matter of much more easy attainment under the New, prefigured by Josue, under whose guidance the people of Israel entered the promised land.

SEVENTH DIFFICULTY.—Are we not justly horrified at the words of Isaias "that Hell hath enlarged her soul and opened her mouth without any bounds?"[61]

Answer.—Duhamel says that by *Hell* in this passage is meant the tomb; and Tirinus says that it may be understood either of hell itself or of the graveyard.

Cornelius à Lapide quotes Sanchez in support of interpreting hell in this passage to mean the common

---

[58] "In the wilderness shall your carcasses lie. All you that were numbered from twenty years old and upwards [stated in Numb. i. 46, and Exodus xxxviii. 25, at 603,550 men], and have murmured against Me, shall not enter into the promised land except Caleb . . . and Josue" (Numb. xiv. 29, 30).

[59] Numb. xxvi. 51.

[60] Chap. xiv. 29.

[61] Isaias v. 14.

Solution of Difficulties. 105

burying-place of the Jews, situated in that part of the valley of Cedron, called, as we learn from the Fourth Book of Kings,[62] Gehenna, or Tophet. If this last interpretation be correct, the meaning of the passage in question is, that so prodigious would be the massacre of the Jewish people of every rank, and so numerous the bodies of the dead that the common burying-place Gehenna would not contain them within its thin limits, but would have to be considerably enlarged for the purpose.

In like manner Jeremias prophesies that the Jews should be all buried in that graveyard, because they had there sacrificed their children to Moloch.[63]

The fifth chapter of Isaias here quoted is altogether concerned with temporal punishments, of a very aggravated kind certainly, and therefore this interpretation seems correct if the passage be taken in its literal sense. But even were we to understand the word Hell to mean in this passage the final abode of the wicked, why should we be astonished at the prophet's writing in a manner well suited to convey an adequate notion of the vast multitudes doomed to perdition in the times whereof he was speaking, when the whole generation of men, not excepting the Jews themselves, were steeped in idolatry and vice of every description?

As for the rest, if this text were to be taken in the general without reference to some particular period of history, and to the nature of the punishment indicated, there would be no small difficulty in reconciling it with

---

[62] 4 Kings xxiii. 6.

[63] "And they have built the high places of Tophet, which is in the valley of the son of Ennom, to burn their sons and their daughters in the fire. . . . Therefore behold the days shall come, saith the Lord, and it shall no more be called Tophet, but the Valley of slaughter. And they shall bury in Tophet because there is no place" (Jerem. vii. 31, 32).

another text from the same prophet, wherein he says that the gates of the Heavenly Jerusalem shall be open day and night,[64] a passage which of course alludes to the gates of Paradise, as plainly appears from the eighteenth and following verses of chapter lx., and also from the corresponding passage in the Apocalypse: "The gates thereof shall not be shut by day.[65]

EIGHTH DIFFICULTY.—How is it possible to suppose that the number of the saved shall be many, when Isaias says they shall be few as the remnant of olives that fall from the olive-tree when it is shaken, or as the grapes that are gleaned after the vintage.[66]

Answer.—In his explanation of this passage, St. Jerome says that it clearly refers to the coming of Antichrist, when, under the pressure of dreadful persecution, few shall be found steadfast in faith.[67]

Cornelius à Lapide accepts this explanation as exclusively correct, and Mgr. Martini, Calino, Menochius, and Tirinus adopt it as the only true interpretation.

Duhamel attributes two meanings to the passage; he says it refers either to the time when Thelgathphalnasar had carried off several of the ten tribes of Israel,[68] or to the coming of Antichrist, when, according to the expla-

---

[64] "And thy gates shall be open continually; they shall not be shut day nor night" (Isaias lx. 11).

[65] Apoc. xxi. 25.

[66] "As if a few olives that remain should be shaken out of the olive-tree, or grapes when the vintage is ended" (Isaias xxiv. 13).

[67] "When the curse shall devour the earth . . . so few shall be the saints, and so great the persecution of the just, that, if it be possible, even the elect of God shall be seduced, and their fewness in number be compared to the rare olive berry that remains on the topmost branches, and to the few grapes which the poor are wont to glean when the vintage is done" (St. Jerome's commentaries on this passage).

[68] 1 Paralip. v. 26.

nation of St. Jerome, as given above, few would remain steadfast in faith.

To hold, on the other hand, this prophecy to mean that all the olive and grape harvest is to be given to Lucifer, and the gleanings alone reserved for Christ, would reduce to a mere mockery of Jesus Christ that other prediction of the same Prophet, which, as interpreted by Mgr. Martini, is a promise by the Eternal Father to His Son that, because the soul of Jesus Christ had laboured, He should see abundant fruit of His toils, and His mighty hunger and thirst for the salvation of souls should be satisfied, and that all the nations of the earth should become His inheritance.[69]

Moreover, it is worthy of remark that in all the parables uttered by Jesus Christ the just are always symbolized by good and superior objects, and the wicked by bad and inferior sorts ; as we see in the parable of the fishes, and in that of the wheat and tares. Is it likely, then, that the ordinary style of Scripture should be departed from in this solitary text, and the wicked be therein compared to the good olives and grapes that had been culled and garnered, and the just to the scanty, sour, and unripe fruit which is usually left for the gleaner ?

NINTH DIFFICULTY.—Jesus Christ Himself warns us that " wide is the gate and broad is the way that leadeth to destruction, and many there are who go in thereat," and on the other hand that " few there are who find the way which leadeth to salvation."[70] It follows that, if

---

[69] "Because His soul hath laboured, He shall see and *be filled*: therefore will I distribute to Him very many" (Isaias liii. 11, 12).

[70] "Wide is the gate and broad is the way that leadeth to destruction, and many there are who go in thereat. . . . Strait is the way that leadeth to life, and few there are that find it" (St. Matt. vii. 13, 14).

many go into the way of destruction and few find the way of salvation, many more shall be lost than shall be saved.

Answer.—In the first place we concur in the observation of Calino,[71] that whenever Holy Writ seems to limit the number of the saved to a minority, it includes in its reasoning Gentiles, Jews, schismatics, heretics, and bad Catholics. Now all men are journeying to eternity, and the road to destruction not being, as St. Bernard remarks, fenced in by any religious bounds or precepts, and being, as Mellifluus has it, rather an open country than a road properly so called, all vices, superstitions, and sects freely traverse its wide expanse, and it is not to be wondered at that it should be called wide and broad, and that many should be said to enter thereon. [72] So also says the Venerable Father Louis da Ponte.[73]

Furthermore, Calino bids us observe that when Christ told us that the way of destruction is wide and broad and trodden by many, He said not that many walk on it until death, but that many go in thereat; the reason being that of the many who in their youth go in through the gate, and for a period walk in the way of destruction, numbers, after having been borne with by our Lord for a time, are converted by the influence of His many-sided grace, reform their lives on the Christian model, and are saved.

But even, continues Calino, if we were to explain the texts in question to point to the small number of the saved, we must understand them as spoken with a refer-

---

[71] *Les. Sacre*, t. iv. n. 10, Serm. xxi.

[72] "Neither is the way a broad way. For straightness is an apt description of a way; broadness of a plain, rather than of a way. A lonely road is wide enough, and the space where no road is, is all a road. Thus the way is open to all vices, having the widest limits, namely, no limits at all" (St. Bern. *De fallac. præs. vitæ*).

[73] *Voce Divina*, cap. i. § 4, p. 65.

ence to some particular time or under some implied condition; for without some such understanding they exhibit a decided discrepancy with other texts.

For instance, though Jesus Christ says in the texts before referred to, "but few are chosen," and "few there are that find it"—that is, the way leading to life—yet in another place, in St. Matthew, we find Him saying, "Many shall come from the east and the west, and shall sit down with Abraham, and Isaac, and Jacob in the Kingdom of Heaven."[74]

Now, how are these two sets of texts to be reconciled? If "few are chosen," if "few find the way to life," how comes Jesus afterwards to say, "Many shall come . . . and shall sit down in the Kingdom of Heaven?" How can the many be few, or the few many? How can the just be "multiplied beyond the sand?"[75]

Let us, therefore, distinguish between the times when these several utterances were delivered, and all discrepancy between them will disappear. In the first, Jesus Christ was speaking of His own time on earth, and of the few that should then be converted; therefore He said that few find the way to salvation, "few there are that find it." Mark, He says not that it shall always be so, "few there shall be that find," but, as Salmeron notices,[76] "few there are." In the second, when Jesus was adverting to the numbers who should, after His death, be converted and saved through the ministry of the Apostles, He no longer speaks of the few, but proclaims, on the contrary, that "many shall come and shall sit . . . in the Kingdom of Heaven" in the times that were to be. In like manner David foretold, with reference to the same times, that the friends of God, in

[74] St. Matt. viii. 11.
[75] "They shall be multiplied above the sand" (Psalm cxxxviii. 18).
[76] Tom. iv. tract. 13, p. 2.

other words the elect, should be "multiplied above the sands of the sea," yea, "that all the ends of the earth would be converted to the Lord, and all the kindred of the Gentiles should adore in His sight." [77]

No wonder, then, that St. John the Evangelist saw not a few, but a countless multitude of saints from all nations and tribes and peoples and tongues.[78]

TENTH DIFFICULTY.—But how fearful is the language of the holy Fathers on this subject! How can sinners ever hope to be saved, bearing in mind St. Jerome's saying, "that out of a hundred thousand such sinners, scarce one merits pardon of his sin from God." [79]

Answer.—It is quite true that St. Jerome says that scarcely one merits pardon; but we must observe that he is not speaking of all sinners without distinction; he makes express and exclusive reference to those who had always led a wicked life. Now although the class who lead a wicked life are far too numerous, there are not many who are not from time to time visited by thoughts of amendment, and who are not converted from the heart by some extraordinary influences set in motion by our Lord for that purpose. Of such as these it cannot be absolutely said, in the language of the holy Doctor, that they have *always* led a wicked life up to the hour of death.

---

[77] "I will number them, and they shall be multiplied above the sand" (Psalm cxxxviii. 18). "All the ends of the earth shall be converted to the Lord; and all the kindred of the Gentiles shall adore in His sight" (Psalm xxi. 28).

[78] "I saw a great multitude, that no man could number, of all nations, and tribes, and peoples, and tongues" (Apoc. vii. 9).

[79] "Of 100,000 sinners that have *always* led a bad life, scarcely one ever merits the attainment of indulgence from God" (St. Jerome).

As little can we infer from these words of St. Jerome that he is of opinion that few shall be saved; for in his exposition of the sentence "few are chosen," he says it alludes to the few Catholics who shall remain steadfast to their faith in the time of Antichrist,[80] and he founds his argument for so believing on the context itself of the parable of the labourers in the market-place, who received their calls at different hours of the day. The persons called during those hours—the hours signifying, according to St. Gregory[81] and others, the five great stages in the world's history, namely, from Adam to Noe, from Noe to Abraham, from Abraham to Moses, from Moses to Jesus Christ, and from Jesus Christ to the end of the world—such persons, I say, are many, "many are called," and the elect, namely, those who preserve their faith inviolate through the unhappy times of Antichrist, are few, "but few are chosen." And here we may reflect, in passing, on the goodness of God, Who has declared that those days of horror and persecution[82] shall be shortened for no other reason than to put a limit to the number of the lost; so that if, according to received opinion, all the Jews shall be at this conjuncture converted, there is all the more reason to hope that many persons who had lapsed from the faith during the short period of persecution, shall also be converted and, escaping its effects, be saved.

---

[80] "There being but few men left when the curse shall have devoured the earth, . . . so rare shall be the number of the saints, of whom the Lord speaks in the Gospel of St. Matthew xx. 16 ('Many are called and few chosen'), that they may be compared to the excessively few olive berries which, after the branches have been shaken and the harvest gathered, remain on the topmost boughs" (*Comm. on Isaias* xxiv. 13).

[81] Lib. i. Hom. xix. n. 1. Edit. Maur.

[82] "For the sake of the elect those days shall be shortened" (St. Matt. xxiv. 22).

ELEVENTH DIFFICULTY.—St. John Chrysostom, speaking of the populous city of Antioch, said that a hundred people who should be saved could not be found among all the thousands of its inhabitants, nay, that he even doubted whether there were so many.[83] When the disproportion of the saved to the lost is so great, how can any one flatter himself that he shall be one of the smaller number?

Answer.—It would be sufficient to say in reply that, considering how Antioch teemed with multitudes of idolaters, Arians, Pelagians, Semi-Pelagians, and bad Catholics, the holy Doctor was justified in endeavouring to rouse them to terror and repentance by a representation of the comparatively small number amongst them worthy of salvation. If, however, the whole of his Homily be read with attention, we shall see that the great object which the holy prelate [84] had in view in writing it was to impress on the Christians the far greater need they had of reforming their lives, than for indulging in vain boasts about the increase of their numbers.

By the example of purity of life many might have been drawn into the Church, and hence he mourns over the absence of morality and living holiness among the generality of the baptized. Moreover, as very many of the Christians had been drawn into the vortex of sin which overspread that populous city, he asks them, How many of our citizens, think you, shall be preserved? and with

---

[83] "Out of so many thousands a hundred cannot be found worthy of salvation; nay, even do I doubt if there be so many" (Hom. xl. *De Pœnit.* p. 100).

[84] "For if the present members of the Church were only conspicuous for the purity of their lives, multitudes of converts would flock in. But if the present members are the reverse, the multitude of real converts will never come" (Tom. iii. Hom. xxiv. *In Act. Apost.* Edit. Paris, 1614).

Solution of Difficulties. 113

sorrow he answers his own question by saying, Scarcely one in a hundred, if indeed so many.[85]

It is obvious, indeed, from the whole context, that the object of the holy prelate was to prove that very few had remained faithful to their baptismal vows, or retained the grace which they had received in the waters of Baptism.[86]

Now as not only the innocent, but the truly penitent are saved, the passage from St. John Chrysostom, thus explained, affords no ground for saying whether the saved are few or many.

Besides, the Saint here speaks as an orator, and uses that exaggeration of expression which is permissible on such an occasion, and is sometimes employed in order to

---

[85] "How many think you in this city shall be saved? It is painful for me to say what I am about to utter. Still I will speak. There are perhaps a hundred to be found in this city who shall be saved; and even of them I have my doubts" (l.c.).

[86] The text of the twenty-fourth homily of the third volume, which is the most authentic, contains the words "they shall be preserved," and "it shall be preserved," as given above, and not "shall be made safe," or "shall be saved," as some ascetic writers hold to be the correct reading. In the same way a "hundredth part," and not "a hundred," is the more authentic reading, as may be seen by reference to the fortieth homily of the fifth volume. This homily is along with others found in the *Anthology*, and is moreover quite different from the translation of the twenty-fourth, vol. iii., as will easily be seen on a comparison of the two. It must also be remarked that it was a common practice among ascetic writers to substitute "a hundred" for "a hundredth part." The meaning therefore of St. Chrysostom is, that one per cent., or the hundredth part of 100,000, namely, 1,000 and not 100 should be preserved. Lastly, take note that many editors and translators throw a doubt upon the authorship of many of these homilies, and hesitate to ascribe them to St. John Chrysostom, and among the rest on this twenty-fourth homily, which they say is unlike in style to that ordinarily adopted by this learned writer. Tricallet, in the analysis which he makes of the Saint's works, speaks of various other homilies, but makes no allusion to this particular one.

I

strike the audience with terror, and to rouse them from their apathy touching salvation. After all, he does not enunciate his proposition as a certainty or a revelation from God, but speaks of it doubtingly, and we are therefore justified in not accepting it in all its rigour.

Finally, it should be remembered that his observation is not applicable to the Catholics only, but that it refers also to the multitude of heretics and infidels included among the inhabitants of the entire city of Antioch.

TWELFTH DIFFICULTY. — Though there may be a doubt as to the meaning of St. John Chrysostom, there can be none as to what St. Gregory means when he says, "Many come to the faith, but few are led onward to salvation," following it up with the exclamation, "who is there that can tell how few are they that are reckoned in the fold of the chosen?"[87]

Answer.—No doubt the language of St. Gregory is here plain enough; but if the proofs which he adduces in support of his words are attentively considered, it will be at once seen that texts such as this one cannot without a manifest inconsistency be taken to imply that only a few are saved.

In fact, for proof of his assertion to that effect, he gives as a reason the following: "At the voice of God the faithful are multiplied exceedingly, because *sometimes* they *also* come to the faith, who do not afterwards succeed in being numbered among the chosen."[88] Now,

---

[87] "Many come to the faith, but few are led onward to the Kingdom of Heaven. . . . How few the numbers are [that are reckoned in the fold of God's elect, who can tell?" (Hom. xix. *In Matt.* cap. xx. tom. ii. p. 110).

[88] "For at the call of God the faithful are multiplied exceedingly: because sometimes persons also come to the faith who do not attain to the ranks of the chosen" (l.c. D).

in order to justify the meaning which gives rise to the difficulty, this last quoted passage should run not "because sometimes," but because *many times* or rather *very many times* (if we wish to preserve the true contrast with the preceding "how few"), they *also* who come to the faith, do not afterwards succeed in being numbered among the chosen. With the same view likewise, the adverb *also* should be omitted from the passage, for this word implies that infidels and others—who do not come to the faith—are included among those who do not succeed in being numbered among the chosen.

Let it not be urged, on the other hand, that his discourse referred to his auditors within the Church, and therefore to the faithful alone; for although he says, "behold how many flock to this day's festival, we fill the church to the very walls." Yet in the exclamation with which he concludes his discourse, he no longer uses the pronoun indicative of the first person plural—for had he used it he could have meant only his audience then present—but the pronoun indicative of the third person, as thus, "And yet who is there that can tell how few are they that are numbered in the flock of the chosen of God." And although it might be thought that we are to understand this passage as if it were written, "who is there that knows how *few of us*," still as he has omitted the words *of us*, and concluded with the third person, his language is wide enough to include, without introducing any contradiction to the general sense, those who were outside the congregation. Moreover by giving this extended meaning to his words, we avoid the inconsistency which, under a different interpretation, would exist, as we before observed, between his naked assertion and the reason he gives in support of it.

And if it be a rational canon of criticism that we should use a text free from all obscurity to throw light on one that is obscure, the two passages above cited from St. Gregory ought to be construed in that sense which is consistent with the proof he brings forward to support them.

But this interpretation, moderate as it is, does not go the whole extent to which the holy Doctor carried his views. We see this from his exposition on another occasion of the parable from which he extracted the saying, "Many are called, but few are chosen." In that exposition he distinctly lays down that the labourer's daily hire in the parable must be taken to mean life eternal; and he goes on to show how all, notwithstanding the disparity in their respective merits and glory, may receive this same daily hire, without in the slightest degree contravening the saying of Jesus Christ, that in His Father's house "there are many mansions." Now, is it not clear from this exposition given by the holy Doctor,[89] that in his opinion the parable in question concerns those only who are saved, including in that category as well those who are called as those who are chosen? How can his interpretation of the daily hire, namely, that it means eternal life and is given to all who are called, consist with any other supposition?

We are therefore forced to the conclusion that the object of the holy Pontiff was to awaken in his hearers the spirit of humility, and fervour in good works, from considerations drawn from the uncertainty of their being chosen although called, and from the

[89] "Whence our Lord says: 'In My Father's house are many mansions.' And yet those who were introduced into it, although arriving at different hours, have received the same hire. How then can the many mansions consist with the one hire, unless because, ... whilst the mead of joy dealt out to each one varies, all share in the one great joy of the vision of Him Who hath made that house" (Hom. xvi. *In Ezech*. p. 83, C).

insufficiency of faith, as infused merely at Baptism, for guaranteeing their salvation. For this reason he made a wide application of the Gospel maxim, "Many are called but few are chosen,"[90] whereby he inclined his audience to understand it in a more strict, but no doubt a Catholic, sense, although, as we have shown, a sense in which he did not himself concur. He adopted this course, because in mere matters of opinion, where opinions conflict, it is not only permissible to enforce, but zeal for the salvation of souls dictates the duty of enforcing that particular opinion which under the circumstances appears the most profitable for their welfare.

And here let us remark the gentle spirit animating the holy Doctor, for being apprehensive that by his warnings against presuming on faith alone, and by his exhortations to good works, he might have excited in the minds of his auditors too keen a sense of terror, he bade them remember the infinite power of God's mercy in the matter of the conversion of sinners, which should prevent them from despairing of the salvation of any one.[91] This declaration of his sentiments alone, shows decisively that he did not favour the opinion that the number of those who attained salvation through the mercy of God was very small.

THIRTEENTH DIFFICULTY.—St. Anselm also says that "there are few who are saved."[92]

[90] "There are two matters which should be ever present to our thoughts. For since many are called but few are chosen, the first is that no one should presume on himself, for although called to the faith, he is ignorant whether he be worthy of the eternal kingdom" (Hom. xix. *In Evang. Matt.* xx. tom. ii. E, p. 120).

[91] "The second is that, ignorant as we are of the treasures of Divine mercy, no one ought to despair of his neighbour, however deeply he may see him steeped in vice" (*Ibid.*).

[92] "As appears the number of the saved are few" (*In elucid.*).

Answer.—As to the saying of St. Anselm, we need only briefly remark that we can conclude nothing from this utterance of his; for, even if it conveyed his own unqualified opinion, he would not have with him the unanimous concurrence of all the other holy Fathers; and also because he does not make the assertion positively but introduces it with the expression "as it seems." Moreover his observation includes the whole mass of mankind.

FOURTEENTH DIFFICULTY.— Has not God Himself desired substantially to confirm us from time to time in the opinion that very few should be saved, by many and terrible visions. For instance, Father Paul Segneri narrates how a damned soul, one month after death, appeared to the Archbishop of Paris and told him that "souls fell into hell thick as snow-flakes in mid-winter on the earth." [93]

Cornelius à Lapide also narrates that a hermit once appeared to the Bishop of Langres, and told him that the same hour which saw him pass to another life, witnessed the death of 30,000 persons, among these being St. Bernard, who together with himself was transported into Heaven, that three were consigned to Purgatory, and all the rest plunged into Hell.

Lastly the same author describes to us the vision of St. Simon Stylites, confirmed by St. Nilus, wherein it was shown to him that in those times "scarcely one out of every ten thousand was saved."

Answer.—It is but too true that there exists immense multitudes of heretics, schismatics, infidels, and bad Catholics, and it may well have happened that, in order to strike sinners with terror, and bring about their conversion, our Lord may have, after some sanguinary

[93] Tom. ii. pred. 14, n. 9, p. 126.

battle or destruction of the infidels' fleet, revealed in vision the headlong flight of their souls to hell. But we are not therefore to infer that souls, and especially Christian souls, are always descending thither in like multitudes. In point of fact we read in the life of St. Catharine of Racconigi, that after the battle fought at Ceresole in Piedmont, where about 10,000 Piedmontese had been left dead upon the field, very few of them were eternally lost, as previously to the fight the whole army had just made their Paschal confession.

We also read in the life of St. Margaret of Cortona, that Jesus Christ commissioned the Saint to bid the Friars Minor remember the souls in Purgatory, numerous beyond the power of imagination to conceive. But if so very few souls had been habitually sent thither by God for the purging away of their sins, how could they possibly have been there in such numbers? We may also set against these peculiar visions of horror, the great fact that there have been occasions from time to time when countless hosts of holy martyrs ascended straight from earth to Heaven; take for instance those who by thousands are commemorated on the 6th of October and the 3rd of November, as well as on many other days, as may be seen by reference to the Roman Martyrology,[94] and ecclesiastical history. Thus, for example, it is related by Nicephorus, that 20,000 Christians were burned by Diocletian on a certain Christmas Day.[95]

[94] "Treviris commemoratio innumerabilium pene martyrum. Cæsaraugustæ sanctorum innumerabilium martyrum," &c.

[95] The journal, *La France Chrétienne*, in its 180th number, and second year, towards the close, contains a table of statistics, copied from the Neapolitan journal, *Eco della verità*. According to this table, the population of the world amounts to 632 millions, which, on an average of 34 years to individual life, would give the deaths at only 35 per minute. According to Sturm's calculation (*Consideration sur Dieu*, t. i. p. 294), the population of the world would

FIFTEENTH DIFFICULTY.—Even though we should admit that the majority of Christians are saved, nevertheless when we remember the maxim, "that outside the Catholic Church there is no salvation," and reflect on the vast disproportion existing at all times between Catholics and heretics, schismatics, and infidels, the number of the saved is reduced almost to zero. This consideration would lead to the conclusion that God is indifferent to the salvation of mankind; and our human nature revolts against belief in a religion, one of whose tenets is, that God, though infinitely good in His essence, has created men for no other end than eternal damnation. And yet it is clearly laid down in the Gospel, "He that believeth not shall be condemned," whilst the Church also says, "that no one can be saved who does not hold the Catholic faith."[96]

Answer.—First take the case of heretics and schismatics. Now a great number coming under this category are not, except in mere form, outside the Church, in consequence of their ignorance not being culpable. To this class belong those who, having received the sacrament of Baptism, are thereby admitted into the Catholic Church, from whose pale no one after admission is ever expelled, who, as St. Liguori lays down in his works *De præcepto fidei*,[97] and *Quid sit hæresis*,[98] with the full

amount to 1,080 millions, and taking the average of life at 33 years, 32,727,727 persons would die every year; 2,727,310 every month; 90,910 every day; 5,787 every hour; and 63 every minute. Now supposing the population were doubled, the mortality would not exceed 7,594 per hour. But if, in accordance with the vision narrated above, souls are continuously falling into Hell, thick as snowflakes in winter, or leaves in autumn, very many millions would be precipitated into the infernal abyss every second, and every hour a number perfectly incalculable, in other words, far more than exist on the face of the earth.

[96] St. Mark xvi. 16; Symb. St. Athan. v. 1.
[97] Cap. iv. dub. 3.
[98] N. 17.

knowledge of error, does not obstinately persist in it. This doctrine derives support from St. Augustine,[99] who says in his writings on Baptism,[100] and against Donatus,[101] that those who do not pertinaciously uphold a false and pernicious doctrine, especially where they are not themselves the authors of the error, but have inherited it from erring and perverted parents—in a word, those who in all sincerity seek after truth, and are ready to embrace it when found ("are ready to be corrected when they shall find the truth"), cannot by any means be reckoned among the number of heretics. St. Fulgentius,[102] speaks to the same effect; and Nicole[103] himself says, that such as have not voluntarily and with a full knowledge of what they were about, gone into schism or heresy, are to be reckoned as children of the Catholic Church.

Hence there are good grounds for hoping that many, classed as schismatics and heretics, will, no other obstacle intervening, be saved, just as if they had formally declared themselves to be Catholics.

Next as to the case of infidels. According to the Angelical Doctor,[104] the observance of the Hebrew law was not, prior to the Gospel, obligatory on infidels. Before this period faith in God as Creator and Remunerator was, in addition to the observance of the law of nature, essential to all in order to salvation, but not so an explicit belief in a Redeemer to come. Explicit belief in such a Redeemer was required only from those

---

[99] St. Augst. tom. ii. Epist. clxii. *Contra Don. pertinaciam.* Paris Edit. p. 277.
[100] Cap. xxv. n. 73.
[101] Cap. iv. n. 5, &c.
[102] Lib. *De Fide ad Petrum*, cap. xxxix.
[103] *Traité de l'unité de l'Eglise*, liv. ii. cap. iii.
[104] 1. 2. q. 98, art. 5.

to whom the promise had been made or communicated. Implicit belief in the faith of the Fathers was all that was required from others.[105]

In point of fact, among these others were Melchisedech and Job, who observed the natural law, believed in God and a Redeemer to come, and attained salvation without any of the canonical practices of the Jewish Law.

Since the advent of Jesus Christ, in addition to explicit faith in God as Creator and Remunerator, faith in the mysteries of the Trinity and of the Incarnation is an essential to all in order to salvation; explicit faith to those to whom the Gospel has been sufficiently promulgated; an implicit faith to those to whom the Gospel has not been so promulgated.

This being premised, as God wishes that every man should be saved, and arrive at the knowledge of truth,[106] namely, Jesus Christ—as He Himself pronounced that He was[107]—and as Jesus Christ is the true light that enlighteneth every man without exception, He never at any time has failed, and never will fail, to supply every one who does not himself present opposing obstacles, with the aids necessary for salvation. This is the concurrent teaching of St. Denis,[108]

---

[105] "Some however, like children, placed implicit faith in what their fathers believed" (In 3 *Sent. Dist.* 25, q. 2, art. 2, ad 2 quæst.).

[106] "God will have all men to be saved, and to arrive at the knowledge of the truth" (1 Tim. ii. 4).

[107] "I am the truth" (St. John xiv. 6). "He was the true light that enlighteneth every man that cometh into the world" (i. 9).

[108] "For before the nations, amongst whom we are, is expanded an immense and boundless sea of Divine light, which is ever burning, and ever open to be partaken of by all" (*De Cœlesti Hierarchiâ*, cap. ix.).

Solution of Difficulties.

St. John Chrysostom,[109] St. Prospero,[110] and St. Thomas.[111]

In point of fact, all men can and, according to the measure of each one's capacity, ought by the sole light of reason to arrive at the knowledge of God, the Author and Preserver of all things; for from visible things are understood the invisible, yea, even the omnipotence and perfections of God.[112] They are also aware of their obligations to observe the law of nature written on their hearts, their own consciences accusing or defending them, so that they who do not observe it are, as St. Paul says, without excuse, for they are amply supplied with the aids required to enable them to do so.[113]

---

[109] "Grace has been shed over all; neither Jew, nor Greek, nor barbarian, nor Scythian, neither freeman nor slave, neither male nor female, neither old nor young, are excepted nor cast away. Whosoever neglects to avail himself of the gift . . . shall bring down punishment on his own head. For, since access is afforded to all, and no one is excluded, his own malice alone can prevent any one from entering" (Hom. *In Joan.*).

[110] "We have laboured to show . . . that not alone *in those latter days*, but in all bygone ages, the grace of God was present, by different modes of operation, and in different measures indeed, but with equal providence, to all men" (St. Prosp. lib. ii. *De voc. Gent.* cap. xxxi.).

[111] "In all things necessary to salvation, God is never, and never has been, wanting to the man seeking after salvation, unless indeed he lag behind through his own fault" (St. Thomas in 3 *Sent. Dist.* xxv. q. 2, ar. 1 ad 1, et ar. 2 ad 2 q.).

[112] "For by the greatness of the beauty, and of the creatures, the Creator of them may be known" (Wisdom xiii. 5). "For the invisible things of Him from the creation of the world are clearly seen; being made known by the things that are made: His eternal power also and His Divinity, so that they are inexcusable" (Rom. i. 20).

[113] "For when the Gentiles, who have not the law, do by nature the things that are of the law, these not having the law are a law to themselves, who show the law written in their hearts, their conscience bearing witness to them, and their thoughts between themselves accusing or also defending one another" (Rom. ii. 14, 15).

Even Jean Jacques Rousseau admits this truth.[114]

The knowledge thus acquired prompts men to have recourse to God, in order to do Him honour, and to call on Him for a share in His bounty, and for those helps necessary to enable them to act rightly, and learn the Divine will, and the form of worship God approves. If men respond to these promptings, and the other helps sent from God, by prayer and the due observance of the natural law, so far as is in their power, it is to be believed with "entire certainty,"[115] as the Angelical Doctor affirms, that God will not fail to reveal to them the truths necessary for salvation, by means either of direct inspiration, or an angelical messenger, or preacher of the Gospel, sent as Peter was to Cornelius; or finally, by some other means which, as Bergier says,[116] God reserves to Himself and is under no obligation to disclose to us.

In this manner God acted on the Gentiles of old, who, as St. Denis tells us,[117] were taught by the angels who had each the special charge of a particular nation. Job[118] gives us similar information concerning his friends,

---

[114] *Emil.* t. iii. Edit. Amst. 1762, pp. 69, 104, 107.

[115] "If one, bred up in the wood, should follow the guidance of natural reason in seeking after good and flying evil, it is a matter to be believed with perfect certainty, that God will either reveal to him what is necessary to be believed, or He will send to him some preacher of the faith, as he sent St. Peter to Cornelius" (St. Thomas, q. 14, *De Veritate*, ar. 11 ad 1).

[116] L.c. p. 256.

[117] "Nempe in aliis Gentibus . . . ad immensum . . . pelagus; ad quod sane obsequenter ducebunt angeli præpositi singulis Gentibus" (*De Cælesti Hierarchia*, cap. ix.).

[118] "There stood one whose countenance I knew not, an image before my eyes, and I heard a voice as it were of a gentle wind" (Job iv. 16). "By a dream in a vision by night when deep sleep falleth on man, then he openeth the ears of men and teaching instructeth them what they are to learn" (xxxiii. 15 16).

whom he describes as taught in sleep by visions of the night; and Leibuzio himself, in one of his letters to Father Grimaldi,[119] admits this doctrine, and says, moreover, in his *Theodicea*,[120] that God will even, if necessary, by miraculous intervention give the knowledge of Jesus Christ to those unbelievers who do all that, humanly speaking, lies in their power. He goes on to say that it is impossible for us to know what passes in the soul at the point of death, whilst God has open to Him the whole infinitude of means, which He can draw on either for the purposes of justice or mercy; and all that can be said to the contrary amounts to this, that we are in ignorance of the means which the Almighty employs to compass His end.

From the foregoing Bergier admirably concludes, and in so doing he states the doctrine of the Catholic Church (as is proved by the fifth of the propositions condemned by Alexander VIII., and also by the condemned propositions, twenty-six, twenty-seven, and twenty-nine, of Quesn.)[121] that no heretic, pagan, Jew, or the like, is absolutely excluded from the benefit of redemption, because by virtue of the merits of Jesus Christ, as we before observed,[122] all men at all times have had, and now have, within their reach the means of salvation, which they may either use or abuse at pleasure.

---

[119] Opusc. tom. i. v. p. 75.

[120] Tom. i. p. 92.

[121] "Pagans, Jews, heretics, and others like them, receive no influence from Jesus Christ, and consequently thou mayest rightly infer that their will is left to its own resources without any sufficient grace" (Prop. 5, condemned by Alexander VIII. Decr. December 7, 1690). "No grace is given except through faith" (Prop. 26). "Faith is the first grace and fountain of all others" (Prop. 27). "Outside the Church no grace is granted" (Prop. condemned by Clement XI. in Constit. *Unigenitus*).

[122] Tesoro xxix. p. 272.

And if Bossuet argued[123] that, taking into consideration the dispersion of the Jews throughout the nations, and the numerous miracles worked by God, there is good reason to suppose that many more individuals among the Gentiles worshipped God, and are consequently saved, than is generally thought, how much more forcibly does this same argument apply now-a-days when the Gospel has been preached all the world over.[124] There is then no cause for wonder in St. John's having beheld in Heaven countless multitudes of the blessed of all nations, tribes, peoples, and tongues.[125] St. Peter says that the man who fears God, and acts justly, and well, is acceptable to Him,[126] and should not therefore be deemed outside the pale of the true Church. On the contrary such a man, though not formally professing Catholicity, should be looked on as virtually a Catholic, and consequently on the road to eternal salvation. No one therefore is damned who does not of his own free will resist the graces and lights sent him by God; nd it is with this qualification that we are to understand the maxim that there is no salvation outside the Catholic Church.

In conclusion, says Bergier,[127] whether the number of the saved be few or many, we ought to derive tranquillity of mind, and steadfastness in faith, from the reflection that God cannot do wrong to any one, nor demand an

---

[123] See his works, vol. xxxviii. Edit. Ven. 1789. Two letters to M. Brisacier on M. Coulan's book, *Judicium unius*.

[124] "Their sound hath gone forth into all the earth: and their words unto the ends of the world" (Psalm xviii. 5).

[125] "I saw a great multitude, which no man could number, of all nations, and tribes, and peoples, and tongues" (Apoc. vii. 9).

[126] "In very truth I have found that . . . in every nation he that feareth Him and worketh justice is acceptable to Him" (Acts x. 34, 35.)

[127] L.c.

account save of the talents He has given to each, and that no one can be damned except through his own fault, which must needs be voluntary. Hence it follows that if but few are saved, there are but few who efficaciously desire to be saved, and that if the many die impenitent, it is because they choose to do so.

If damnation were the result of some natural defect, or of the absence of God's help, we should indeed have reason to fear. But God is faithful, and does not permit us to be overcome, or tempted by the enemy, without giving us the grace to resist and confound him to our own great profit.

If salvation depended on chance, we should also have great cause to fear; but it altogether depends on ourselves, and on grace. If we cooperate with grace, we are sure to be saved, as it was to that end we were created, and, as we observed,[128] were provided by God with the means necessary for the attainment of Heaven. Therefore, even if but few were saved, still the devil would not, to use the impious language of Bayle, have reason to triumph over Jesus Christ. On the contrary, even in that case Jesus Christ would be victorious over the devil; for the real victory won by Jesus consists, not in His having rendered it impossible for a man to be damned by his own fault—to have done so would have deprived man of all merit, and consequently of all claim to recompense—but His victory consists in having restored to man the right to Heaven, from which he had been exiled, and the certainty that each one shall, through his Saviour's merits, receive all graces necessary to salvation, so that whoever shall perish is lost without excuse.

In conclusion, even though we be convinced that the number of the saved are many, we ought to be none the

[128] In l.c. t. xxix.

less solicitous about our salvation, always bearing in mind that "no one is crowned except he strive lawfully."[129]

SIXTEENTH DIFFICULTY.—It may be true that adults procure their own damnation, owing to their rejection of the lights and graces sent by God, and their abuse of the means with which He supplies them; but how is it possible to reconcile with the justice, not to say the goodness, of God, His consignment to eternal fire of whole hosts of children, who die without the possibility of being baptized?[130] Can any one, bearing this in mind, believe in the infinite goodness of a God Who creates countless multitudes of human beings, with the sole object of consigning them to everlasting fire, in punishment of original sin, to speak the plain truth, because they had the misfortune to be the children of a guilty father?

Answer.—God not only does no wrong to unbaptized children, but He shows them extraordinary kindness.

And first, Bergier says in reply,[131] God does them no wrong. It would not be deemed contrary to justice to prevent the child of a guilty father from inheriting those privileges which would, but for his crimes, have belonged to that father; so those unbaptized children, though not guilty of what is called actual sin, must needs be tainted in their origin by the primal sin of their great first parent Adam. Hence God denied to all Adam's hapless posterity that grace and glory, and those gratuitous privileges, which would have been his and our delightful portion, had our common ancestor continued in a state

---

[129] 2 Tim. ii. 5.
[130] "Unless a man be born again of water and the Holy Ghost he cannot enter the Kingdom of God" (St. John iii. 5).
[131] *Traité de la Vraie Religion*, tom. ii. pp. 541, 542.

of innocence. And therefore it is that Jesus Christ Himself declared[132] that unless a man be born again of baptism to grace, he cannot enter into the Kingdom of God.

According to Father Natalis Alexander[133] many learned authorities deny that the opinion, that children dying without Baptism are punished with the pains of sense, ever proceeded from St. Augustine, though attributed to him. And if that illustrious Doctor, in the heat of his conflict with the Pelagians, spoke with some asperity as regards the fate of these children, he also elsewhere positively asserts that their punishment was not such as to make it better for them never to have been born; and he adds, thereby confirming his opinion, that their pains shall be of so slight a character that he dare not say that non-existence would be preferable to abiding where they are.[134] Now had he believed that they were condemned to everlasting fire, he never would, says Bergier,[135] have made this assertion, the more especially, remarks Father M. Anfossi, when he had before his eyes the saying of Jesus Christ with respect to a damned soul.[136] For no one surely would prefer existence to non-existence, if his abode were in fire. And of the damned it is

[132] L.c.

[133] *Hist. Eccl.* v. iii. § 10, n. 8.

[134] "I say not that the little ones shall be the prey of such suffering, that it were better for them never to have been born" (tom. vii. lib. v. *In Jul.* cap. viii.). "Who can doubt but the condemnation of these little children shall be the lightest of all, and though I cannot define its nature or extent, yet I dare not say that it would be better for them to be non-existent, than to exist where now they are" (*Ibid.*).

[135] L.c. p. 369, in fine.

[136] "It were better for him, if that man had not been born" (St. Matt. xxvi. 24). Defence of the Bull *Auctorem fidei*, tom. ii. lett. xi. p. 226.

written, that they should seek after death which shall ever fly them; for in death, though long wished for and ardently desired, they shall never find a refuge from suffering.[137]

St. Bonaventure also asserts that St. Augustine did not mean to convey by any expression used by him that unbaptized children were punished by the pains of sense, but referred merely to the pain arising from the privation of the vision of God, and from the wretchedness of their abiding place.[138]

But the illustrious St. Augustine[139] himself removes all doubt as to the sentence which will be passed upon them at the Last Judgment, for he admits it shall be a middle one between reward and punishment; and this opinion he never retracted, although it related to a question which he minutely discussed in his *Retractations*, and especially in Epistle xxvi.

Finally, the Saint solemnly assured St. Jerome in one of his letters that this question about unbaptized children presented such difficulties to his mind, that he was unable to answer it.[140]

Innocent III. and John XXII. affirm in the most distinct terms [141] that unbaptized children are punished

---

[137] "They shall seek death and shall not find it; they shall desire to die and death shall fly from them" (Apoc. ix. 6).

[138] In 2 *Sent. Dist.* xxxiii. a. 3, q. 1, in concl. n. 1.

[139] "There is no fear that there may not be a life intermediate between reward and punishment, just as there is a life intermediate between sin and well-doing" (Lib. iii. *De lib. arb.* cap. xxiii.).

[140] "When I come to the consideration of children, believe me I feel myself pressed by sore straits, nor can I decide upon any answer altogether satisfactory."

[141] "The punishment of original sin consists in the deprivation of the vision of God, but the punishment of actual sin is the torture of everlasting hell" (Innocent. lib. iii. tit. 42, *De Bapt.* cap. iii. § verum). "We believe . . . that the souls of those who die in mortal sin, or only in original sin, at once descend into hell, to suffer in different

Solution of Difficulties. 131

with the pain of loss alone, without undergoing any pain of sense.

The Council of Florence,[142] as the illustrious Father M. Anfossi observes,[143] in no way dissents from the definition laid down by Innocent III. and John XXII.; for the word Hell, occurring in the definition of the Council, must, to preserve consistency in the context, be understood to import a place where the children undergo the pain of loss only, whereas the reprobate are punished there, alike with that pain and the pain of sense.

Next follows the Angelical Doctor,[144] who maintains by the most conclusive reasoning, that original sin does not deserve the pain of sense; inasmuch as sensible pain, according to the rule laid down by St. John in the Apocalypse[145] should bear a proportion to the pleasure derived from the commission of the sin in respect of which it is inflicted; and as original sin imports no pleasure conferred, nor attachment to any created thing, it cannot deserve to be punished by sensible pain."[146]

---

ways and in different places: namely, the soul of children, which shall undergo the pains of loss, but not of sense, in Limbo" (Extract from instructions in the Catholic faith sent to the Armenians in the year 1321, apud Raynald, an. 1321, n. 11).

[142] "We believe . . . that souls which depart in mortal sin, or in original sin alone, at once go down into the world below, but are very differently punished there" (*Conc. Flor.* Sess. vi. an. 1409).

[143] L.c. p. 216.

[144] "The bitterness of sensible bitterness corresponds with the pleasure taken in the commission of sin."

[145] "As much as she hath glorified herself and lived in delicacies, so much torment and sorrow give ye to her" (Apoc. xviii. 7).

[146] "But in original sin there is no turning to the creature, . . . and therefore no pain of sense, but the pain of loss, namely, privation of the Beatific Vision alone, should attend original sin" (*De Malo*, q. 5, ar. 2). "Again, pain of sense is never inflicted on account of mere habitual propensity; for no one is punished because of his capacity for stealing, but solely because he is caught in the act. But some forfeiture attends on habitual deficiency without any

The Seraphic Doctor, St. Bonaventure,[147] having also given his opinion in the affirmative on the first questions, namely, whether unbaptized children are, or are not, exempt from the pain of sense; with regard to the

act done at all, as, for instance, one void of any tincture of letters, would never be deemed worthy of episcopal office. There is however in original sin a certain innate concupiscence acting on habitual inclination, which fits the child to conceive desires, which in the adult issue forth into act. Hence, when the little one dies with the stain of original sin still on him, the pain of loss, but not of sense, should be his portion, since by reason of his lacking original justice, he is rendered unfit for the vision of the Godhead" (*Ibid.*). "It is part however of the knowledge implanted in our nature, that the soul is conscious that she was created in order to be happy, and that happiness consists in the attainment of the perfect good; but that knowledge derived from nature can never tell us that the perfect good for which man was made consists in that glory to which the saints attain according to that of the Apostle—'Eye hath not seen, nor ear heard, neither hath it entered into the heart of man to conceive what God hath prepared for them that love Him;' but God has made known to us by His Spirit the revelation appertaining to faith; and inasmuch therefore as the little ones are in ignorance of what they have forfeited, they mourn not their loss, but enjoy, undisturbed by grief, the goods inherent in their nature" (*Ibid.* ar. 3).

[147] "For this and other reasons a third way of putting the case suggests itself: namely, that the souls of the little ones are exempt from pain and grief, but not from knowledge of the loss. . . . Therefore the souls of these children, placed by the just judgment of God midway between the beatified and the utterly miserable, shall be perfectly sensible of the condition of things, in such sort, that while the prospect on one side gives rise to woe, that on the other applies a balsam; thus by Divine arbitrament are their knowledge and their feelings balanced in opposite scales, . . . but herein is the order of Divine wisdom wonderfully exhibited, which knows how to place everything in the position to which it is suited, and to shape all ends to the glory of God. For as in the blessed mercy chiefly is made manifest, and as justice is made plain chiefly in the damned, so both His mercy and justice are manifested in these little children" (St. Bonav. 2 *Sent. Dist.* xxxiii. in concl. ar. 3. quest 2, E).

second question, namely, whether they are, or are not, exempt from the pain of loss, sets forth the various reasons alleged by those who contend, on the one hand, that they are aware of, and therefore grieve for the good they have forfeited; and on the other, that they have neither knowledge nor grief. The conclusion at which the Saint himself arrives is, that they possess the knowledge, but are exempt from pain, and that their lot is cast midway between the blessed and the reprobate. For he affirms, that to them pain is in equal measure tempered with consolation; so that the Divine Wisdom, which orders all things aright, and shapes all ends to the glory of God, will in an especial manner shine forth resplendent in them. Thus, as the Divine mercy is displayed in the blessed, and the Divine justice in the reprobate, so the Divine mercy and justice are both together manifested in the case of these little ones.

In the second place, God does not fail ever to exercise His goodness on behalf of these little children; for, according to the conclusion arrived at by the Angelical Doctor, from the reasons we have given, and according to the arguments on many other grounds, they are not only exempt from grief for the forfeiture of the Beatific Vision, but they rejoice in being made sharers in the Divine bounty and in the natural perfections with which God has endowed them.[148] Though separated from God to the extent of union in His glory, they are not wholly separated from Him; nay, they are united with Him by participation in those perfections which are communicated to their nature; and thus, by means of their

---

[148] "And therefore they shall feel no kind of grief for the absence of the Beatific Vision, but on the contrary shall greatly rejoice, inasmuch as they shall be made participators of the Divine bounty and natural perfections" (St. Thomas, l.c. ar. 2).

natural knowledge and love, they are enabled to find happiness in God.[149]

The opinions just stated have nothing in common with the error of the Pelagians, which was condemned by Councils, and in the 26th Proposition of the Bull, *Auctorem Fidei*.[150] These heretics altogether denied the existence of original sin in children, and for that special reason—as the Bull *Auctorem* emphatically points out—assign for their abode some middle place or state, exempt from sin and punishment, between Heaven and Hell; whereas we hold, with the Catholic Church, that these children are stained with original sin, and are thereby excluded from the Kingdom of Heaven. And although, according to St. Bonaventure, grief for glory lost has its countervailing balm, and, according to St. Thomas, they not only know not what they have lost and consequently mourn it not, but even, through the medium of created things and by means of natural love and knowledge, they are enabled to rejoice in God Himself; still, we hold, they are undergoing a substantial punishment in the deprivation of a good which, had Adam preserved his

---

[149] "Although unbaptized children are separated from God to the extent of not being united with Him in glory, they are not on that account wholly separated from Him; nay, they are joined with Him by means of enjoying a perfect natural blessedness, and that in such sort that they are able to rejoice in Him with natural knowledge and love" (*Ibid.* art. 5).

[150] "The doctrine which rejects, as though it were a Pelagian fable, the existence of that place in the infernal regions (which believers have always known by the name of the Limbo of children), wherein the souls of those dying in the guilt of original sin only are punished by the pain of loss, unaccompanied by the pain of fire; just as if the very circumstance which exempt from fire should call into existence a place and state midway between the kingdom of God and eternal perdition, exempt alike from punishment and sin—such a place as the Pelagians vainly imagined—this doctrine we say is false, rash, and baneful in Christian schools" (Bulla *Auct. Fidei*, prop. 26).

innocence, would have been gratuitously bestowed on them.

If, then, the action of God in regard to these children be attentively considered, its effect will be, as the Seraphic Doctor says, to lessen their pain if any such they feel. For God, by sending them an early death, conferred on them, especially if they be children of heretics or infidels, the inestimable boon of preservation from many sins, both venial and mortal, and from the countless risks to their salvation which they would have encountered had they lived. Well may we then apply to them the words of Wisdom: "They were taken away by an early death lest wickedness should alter their understanding, or deceit beguile their soul." [151]

And of a truth so great is the boon of preservation from actual sin, that not only they, but we ourselves, ought to prefer a thousand-fold the deprivation of glory to the commission of a single sin.

What reason then have these children for complaint, or in what particular has God wronged them; for though He has not conceded to them the power of attaining to heavenly glory, He has, on the other hand, conceded to them the incalculable benefit of immunity from sin?

Far, therefore, from uttering complaints against God, they ought rather to praise Him, and return Him thanks for His infinite goodness exercised in their behalf.

[151] "He was taken away lest wickedness should alter his understanding" (Wisdom iv. 11).

CHAPTER VIII

Discussion of the question whether, with God's assistance, salvation is of easy or difficult attainment.

FIRST DIFFICULTY.—It is expressly laid down in the Gospel "that the way of salvation is most arduous, and the gate leading to life very narrow;"[1] a consequence, doubtless, of the stringency of the moral code so far above frail, inconstant, and sorely-wounded human nature.

Now, if very few are found willing to face difficulties, and fewer still to bring them, by perseverance, to a successful issue, what is to be said of the difficulty of attaining salvation, which is rendered enormous by the gate leading to life being so narrow that, in the words of the Gospel, "Many seek to enter in but are not able."[2] Add to which that we even do not know what is the nature of the guilt that bars the entrance. If such be the case when our courage to follow after virtue is crushed out of us, and we are thrown into despair at the appalling difficulties that beset us, how can we ever hope to be saved? The conclusion is, that the Christian religion is utterly useless. It offers but infinitesimal advantages, and God has made but a most inadequate

---

[1] "Enter ye in at the narrow gate. . . . How narrow is the gate and strait is the way that leadeth to life, and few there are that find it" (St. Matt. vii. 13, 14).

[2] "Strive to enter in by the narrow gate; for many, I say to you, shall seek to enter, and shall not be able" (St. Luke xiii. 24).

provision for our salvation. No! such a providence cannot be Divine! And yet the Gospel texts, which tell us all this, are too plain to be gainsaid.

Answer.—Bergier, whom we have so often quoted, interprets the narrow gate mentioned by St. Luke to mean the moral code of the Gospel, which prohibits the indulgence of the passions beyond the most rigorous and narrow bounds. He considers that our Lord here meant to use the analogy of what was about to happen at the coming siege of Jerusalem, when many would regret their not having escaped while there was yet time, through the city gates, from the fury of the besiegers. "Strive," was the substance of our Lord's language, "to pass, while there is yet time, through the narrow gate, by giving in your adhesion to My doctrine; for the time is at hand when the besiegers will circle you round about, and you shall rue your not having imitated My disciples in flying betimes from the beleaguered city, by believing in and profiting by My word. Then shall you wish to fly, and shall not be able, but shall perish in one common ruin with Jerusalem.

Duhamel, in his commentary on St. Luke, and Tirinus and Mgr. Martini in their respective expositions of the above-cited passage from St. Matthew, each assert the opinion that by the narrow gate is to be understood the morality of the Gospel, which teaches us how to live virtuously. This conclusion is borne out by the answer given by Jesus to the young man who asked what he should do that he might have life everlasting: "If thou wilt enter into life," answered our Lord, "keep the commandments;" thus signifying that in their observance was the gate by which he could enter in.[3]

Now as the way of the commandments is rugged and

---

[3] "If thou wilt enter into life, keep the commandments" (St. Matt. xix. 17).

strait, to use the expression of St. Gregory the Great,[4] in the eyes of that too numerous class, carnal men; many will strive to enter, in other words, to attain salvation, by the way of their perverse inclinations and passions—a way and gate by which they shall not be able to enter.[5]

The narrowness of the way, and the difficulty of finding it, may be explained by its being confined within the bounds of faith and observance of the commandments; and as the faithful are few in comparison with all others who walk in the way of perdition, so those who find the narrow gate must also be few.[6]

St. Basil [7] expresses similar sentiments, and says that the gate and way to Paradise are not in themselves narrow, but are deemed so only because bounded by certain limits which it is perilous to overstep. The Saint adds that as the traveller who does not keep to the centre of a foot-bridge, but staggers from right to left, probably tumbles into the river, so he who walks not in the straight road of the Divine commandments shall fall into sin and be lost.

St. Gregory the Great also says that this gate and way are not called narrow in themselves, but are so called with reference to the persons who tread and enter them. These consist either of beginners, who find their task, like all beginnings, beset with difficulties; or of proficients, men perfect of life, for whom the road is wide and easy.[8]

---

[4] "It is too confined for the flesh" (Hom. xvii. *In Ezech.*).

[5] "Many, I say to you, shall strive to enter and shall not be able" (St. Luke xiii. 24).

[6] "And few there are that find it" (St. Matt. vii. 14).

[7] *In Regul. Brev.* n. 241.

[8] "For beginners the way is narrow, for the perfect of life it is broad" (Hom. xvii. *In Ezech.*).

St. Diadocus, one of the ancient Fathers cited by St. Maximus, in his interpretation of these passages limits the difficulties of the road to want of familiarity with them on the part of those who enter on it.[9]

St. Augustine in his commentary says: "To the unwilling the way is narrow and toilsome, but to the willing it is broad. As hunting and fishing are to the true sportsman not a toil but a pleasure, for he follows his own bent, so to the loving heart toil is no longer toil but a labour of love." Speaking of the yoke, the same Saint says: "The man who bears it either does not love, in which case he feels it heavy, or he does love, and in that case it cannot but be light."[10]

The way also may be called difficult in order to mark the obstacles to be encountered by the man who designs to walk in the pride of his own strength alone. For such a one indeed the observance of the law of God would be not only a difficulty but an impossibility. This explanation is in conformity with the answer given by Jesus Christ to His disciples, when on hearing Him say that "it is easier for a camel," ("a thick rope" according to others) "to pass through the eye of a needle than for a rich man to enter the Kingdom of Heaven,"[11] they asked with astonishment, "Who can be saved?"[12] Thus they seemed to inquire: if salvation be

---

[9] "To those who begin to love truth, the way of virtue is rough and toilsome: not because it really is so. . . . Therefore whoever has achieved the middle passage will find it smooth and easy" (Lib. *De Perfect. Spir.*).

[10] "Certainly the way is narrow, narrow at least to him to whom walking is a toil, but not to him who loves the road, for nowise are labours of love burdensome, but yield delight, as in the case of the hunter or fisherman" (Lib. *De bono vid.* cap. ii.). "For either man does not love, in which case it is heavy, or he loves, in which case it cannot be heavy" (Lib. *De Nat. et Grat.* cap. lxix).

[11] St. Matt. xix. 24.

[12] St. Matt. xix. 25.

made so difficult, not to say impossible, by an inordinate love of riches,[13] who can be saved in a world wherein there abound many much worse vices? To this question our Lord answered: "With men this is impossible, but with God all things are possible."[14] St. Jerome, in expounding the thirty-second verse of Psalm cxviii.,[15] says, that the so-called rugged road may be made so easy that men may run along its course. And St. Bonaventure observes, that our Lord compares His law to a yoke, the peculiarity of which is that its burthen is always borne by two in conjunction; whereby Christ signifies that we are not alone, and that He Himself helps us in our toil, thus rendering it pleasant and sweet, and making that burthen light which would be insupportable to our own unaided strength.[16]

Our Lord Himself says, by the mouth of Osee, that He will be to us as the prudent husbandman who takes off the yoke from his wearied oxen in order to give them rest;[17] from which passage St. Ambrose in his commentary on the words "I have not laboured following Thee," as they stand in the Septuagint version of Jeremias,[18] takes occasion to say, "to whom can it be a toil to follow Jesus, Who Himself imparts strength to His followers?"[19]

Indeed, no other explanation can be given of the phrase, "Narrow is the gate and strait the way of salvation," without falling into contradiction.

[13] "For them that trust in riches" (St. Mark x. 24).
[14] St. Matt. xix. 26.
[15] "I have run the way of Thy commandments, when Thou didst enlarge my heart" (Psalm cxviii. 32).
[16] "For My yoke is sweet and My burthen light" (St. Matt. xi. 30).
[17] "And I will be as one that taketh off the yoke" (Osee xi. 4).
[18] Cap. xvii. 16.
[19] "Who can labour that follows Jesus, Who imparts strength to His followers."

For to understand the text "Many shall seek to enter and they shall not be able" as meaning in set terms that many may strive to enter, by the observance of the commandments, and the consequent discharge of every duty, and yet not be able to do so, would be to attach a sense to it repugnant to the teaching of the Catholic Church. To do so would be to run counter to the decision of the Council of Trent,[20] which affirms that God does not require impossibilities, and that when He imposes His commands He bids us do our own part to the best of our ability, and seek His aid where our own strength fails.

Again, if we understand this text as meaning that there is very great difficulty attendant on the observance of the commandments, we find ourselves at variance with the Gospel of St. John, who expressly tells us that "the commandments of God are not heavy."[21]

Moreover, if we do not admit the explanation given above from the holy Fathers respecting the words narrow and strait occurring in the text of St. Matthew,[22] namely, that they are to be understood relatively, how can we possibly reconcile that text with the saying of David: "I walked at large, *because* I sought after Thy commandments?"[23] Or with that still clearer saying of the same David: "Thou hast set my feet in a spacious place;"[24] in other words, that God had given him, so to speak, the widest latitude. And be it remembered, that these are the sayings of one who walked in fear, under the law

---

[20] Sess. vi. cap. x.
[21] 1 St. John v. 3.
[22] "How narrow is the gate and strait the way that leads to life" (St. Matt. vii. 14).
[23] Psalm cxviii. 45.
[24] Psalm xxx. 9.

of bondage, as St. Paul says,[25] and not under the law of adoption into the Divine Sonship.

To conclude, if there were any difficulty in the observance of the law of God, what becomes of the promise made by our Lord Himself, that if we take up His yoke we shall find it sweet and pleasant, and its burthen so light that the observance of His law far from being a weary weight, shall bring to our souls peace, tranquillity, and rest.[26]

SECOND DIFFICULTY.—But if St. Peter says, the just man shall scarcely be saved, what then is to become of us poor sinners?[27]

Answer.—Cornelius à Lapide, the Venerable Bede, and St. Augustine, all three wrote commentaries on this text.

Cornelius à Lapide[28] explains it as meaning that if the frailty of corrupt human nature be such that even the just shall not be permitted to enter Heaven, there to receive the crown of glory, without having previously endured tribulation, to purge away all stains contracted here below, how much more of tribulation and distress shall not sinners have to endure?

St. Augustine explains this text in his commentary

---

[25] "For you have not received the spirit of bondage again in fear; but you have received the spirit of the adoption of sons, whereby we cry, Abba, Father" (Rom. viii. 15).

[26] "Take up My yoke upon you . . . and you shall find rest to your souls. For My yoke is sweet and My burthen light" (St. Matt. xi. 29, 30).

[27] "If the just man shall scarcely be saved, where shall the ungodly and sinner appear?" (1 St. Peter iv. 18).

[28] "If the frailty of man be so great, that even the just shall not pass into Heaven to be crowned without enduring tribulation, to purge away the innumerable stains of corrupted nature; how much more must those who are strangers to grace expect the certain issue of their damnation?" (Cornelius à Lapide).

Solution of Difficulties. 143

by asking the question, what is more manifest than that our Lord spares not even the just man, but purifies him by tribulation, since it is written: "If the just man shall scarcely be saved?"[29]

In fine, Cornelius à Lapide adds that the just man shall undoubtedly be saved, but that we must take it that his salvation shall be attained through tribulation, affliction, and chastisements due to venial sins. We are, therefore, to understand the word "scarcely" occurring in the text, to mean with pain and difficulty.

Mgr. Martini adopts the opinion of St. Augustine with regard to this text, and interprets it to mean that the just shall attain salvation through toil, sorrow, and suffering.

THIRD DIFFICULTY.—When we know that many who had reached a high degree of perfection afterwards fell off, and became castaways, have we not also great cause of fear for our salvation? Take for instance Judas: did he not go the length of betraying Jesus Christ, and was he not damned therefore, after he had been a disciple of the Divine Redeemer for full three years, and had even worked miracles? The miserable end of Pelagius is also well known. He had up to a certain point led a life of extreme penance, and was esteemed a saint, but, as narrated by Father Rossignoli[30] was damned for the commission of some heinous sin. Who has not heard also of the fall of Tertullian and Origen, the stately cedars of Lebanon? Ah, well may we exclaim with Zacharias,[31] "Ah, woe to us, weak and miserable, since

---

[29] "What is more evident than that He spares not the just, but corrects them by a variety of tribulations, since it is plainly written with regard to this very subject, 'And if the just man shall scarcely be saved'" (St. Augustine, lib. xx. *Contra Festum*, 14).

[30] *Verità eterne*, &c., Serm. ii. p. 44.

[31] "Howl thou fir-tree, for the cedar is fallen" (Zach. xi. 2).

the cedars of Lebanon, the very pillars of the Church, have fallen!"

Answer.—The number of those who, after a life admired for penance and holiness, have fallen and been condemned, far from being great, is extremely few. Of these few, ascetic writers generally attribute the fall to pride, which, moth-like, consumed their good works, and caused them to substitute hypocrisy for true piety.

As to the case of Judas, the special cause of his condemnation was his despairing of pardon, instead of weeping for his sin, as Peter did for his. By how many ways did not the Lord endeavour to withdraw him from his meditated treachery. Jesus Christ washed his feet, and let him know that He was aware of the treason he was plotting in his mind. Nay, He even endured his kiss in the very act of betrayal, and called him by the endearing name of friend. He reminded him of His power by casting him to the ground along with those who came to effect the arrest, and of His mercy by healing the ear of Malchus. Judas was, in addition, visited by inspirations and promptings of conscience, strong enough to make him confess his crime of betraying his innocent Master, and reject the price of his treason. We may, therefore, conclude that had Judas, like Peter, felt confidence in God, together with repentance, he would, like him, have been admitted to pardon and salvation.

Pelagius also was damned because he so willed it himself. In fact, we are told by Father Rossignoli, that an angel from Heaven came expressly to urge on him the healing virtues of penance. Oh, what remorse of conscience was his! How was he goaded to confess his sin! No one, too, could have been better aware that his severe and multiplied penances availed him nothing, so long as he suffered to remain in his bosom the poison of mortal sin. He also knew full well that every time he approached the sacraments in his state of guilt he added a fresh crime of sacrilege to those already committed, and thus, from the commission of that first sin, his life became one long chain of sacrilegious links, and degenerated into proud hypocrisy, all resulting (as God, according to the authority above cited, forced him to confess), from his fear of forfeiting the reputation for sanctity which he had already gained.

In fine, in all those cases where men have had in life a great repute for sanctity, and been nevertheless damned, the reprobates will turn out on examination to have been hypocrites steeped in pride, and to have well deserved their fate; nor can there be found a single instance of the damnation of one who in sincerity and truth led the life of a good Christian.

FOURTH DIFFICULTY.—Who can tell the number of those who, after having led a life of Christian piety, yield in the hour of death to the furious assaults and temptations of the devil, that devil, be it remembered, who is ever going about like a roaring lion seeking to devour souls?[32] Will he not, when the hour of our death arrives, redouble the rage and fury of his assaults upon us, knowing well how short a time he has to work in? When the last mortal illness weighs us down, when we have no strength to pray, and know not where to turn for aid, how shall we be able to withstand his fierce attacks? Ah, difficult indeed must be the acquisition of salvation, if after successfully braving, as becomes good Christians, the storms of temptation on the sea of life, we have so much reason to fear shipwreck at the very

[32] "Your adversary the devil, as a roaring lion, goeth about seeking whom he may devour" (1 St. Peter v. 8).

mouth of the harbour of safety?[33] Yea, that we shall be at the moment of death sentenced to damnation, like that unhappy one from among the forty martyrs who gave way under the agony of torture, and at the last instant apostatized!

Answer.—Nay; but the very nature of the circumstances stated ought to inspire us with all the more confidence in God. An assassin, bent on murder, and panting for revenge, would be driven to desperation and maddened by fury, if, when in pursuit of his enemy, he saw a favourable opportunity slipping by, and his intended victim drawing near a place of safety, whilst, on the other hand, the object of this malice, if conscious of his danger, would exult in the approach of succour, or in a suddenly descried place of refuge. Just so in the hour of death: in proportion as the devil fumes and foams with rage, because his hour for temptation and persecution is drawing to a close, the more ought we to be buoyed up with courage, and rejoice at our nearing the haven of salvation. True it is that the prospect of being baffled would make the supposed assassin redouble his efforts for the moment. But this consideration should have no terrors for us. For however furious may be the onslaught of the devil, God is faithful,[34] and He has promised that He will not suffer the devil to have all power in his own hands. God indeed permits the devil to tempt us, but He does not permit the devil to overbear by temptation that grace and strength with which He supplies us, in order to enable us to resist our enemy, and convert all his efforts for our destruction into sources of profit. When the last

[33] "The devil is come down unto you, having great wrath, knowing that he hath but a short time" (Apoc. xii. 12).

[34] "God is faithful, Who will not suffer you to be tempted above what you are able to bear, but will also make with temptation issue" (1 Cor. x. 13).

hour comes, God will send aid in proportion to our needs,[35] and though no one, as laid down by the Council of Trent, can *with absolute certainty* promise himself the grace of final perseverance, we may feel an assured confidence, grounded on the certainty of God's assistance, that we shall be saved.[36]

In point of fact, must not God, Who loves us with an infinite love, be more anxious for our salvation than the devil, whose hate, though implacable, is not infinite, can be for our destruction? To suppose that God could abandon us in our sorest need, would it not be the grossest insult to his Divine Majesty? Be assured, exclaims Origen, God's care for our salvation far outstrips that of the devil for our destruction.[37]

A true man would not thus abandon his friend, nor a parent his child, nor a husband the wife of his bosom: and will God abandon us, His friends and children? Will He abandon that soul for whose salvation He shed His Blood, and died upon the Cross? Say not so; but rather let us imitate the confidence of holy David, and say with him, "The Lord is our helper, and we shall look over our enemies; for though we should walk in the midst of the shadow of death, we will fear no evils, for Thou art with us."[38] Remember that "no one hath hoped in the Lord and hath been confounded.[39]

[35] "Where the danger is greatest, there shall the chief aid be given, for God comes to assist us in our emergencies" (St. Ambrose, *De Joseph.* cap. v.).

[36] "Let no one promise himself salvation with absolute certainty; although all should repose the most assured confidence in God" (Sess. vi. cap. xiii).

[37] "God is more anxious to draw us to safety, than is the devil to drive us to perdition" (Hom. xx. *In Lib. Num*).

[38] "The Lord is my helper, and I will look over my enemies" (Psalm cxvii. 7). "Though I should walk in the midst of the shadow of death, I will fear no evil, for Thou art with me" (Psalm xxii. 4).

[39] "No one hath hoped in God, and hath been confounded" Ecclus. ii. 11).

As regards the case of the one individual, who out of a band of forty yielded under the agony of tortures inflicted on account of his faith, and at the last moment apostatized, no doubt he lost the palm of martyrdom, but as ecclesiastical history tells us, the crown which he forfeited was placed upon another head.

And if, according to St. Chrysostom, as before remarked,[40] we have still time, even when we are at the last gasp,[41] to obtain by sincere repentance mercy from God, how much reason is there not to believe that God, compassionating the apostate's weakness, granted him the grace of perfect contrition, and of salvation through that. Thus, though forfeiting the crown of martyrdom, we may believe that he received the reward due to the sufferings endured before his fall, and while he was still in the state of grace. We may not only believe this, but we should admire the goodness of God, Who made his fall the occasion of salvation to the fortunate soldier who had him in charge.

Moreover, if we believe what Blosius says, and the Church[42] approves, namely, that the power and glory of God shine with more conspicuous brightness, the more numerous and malignant the sins pardoned by Him, and the more debased and miserable the sinner whom He has admitted to mercy; how can we sufficiently, continues Blosius,[43] admire and thank the ineffable goodness of our

---

[40] Ch. ii. difficulty 7.

[41] "You have sinned, well, repent. You have sinned ten thousand times, repent ten thousand times. Repent while breath remains, although, so to speak, your soul be departing, and you are passing out of the world, for the shortness of time is no impediment to the exercise of the Divine mercy" (Hom. ii. *In Psalm* l.).

[42] "O God, Who chiefly manifestest Thy almighty power in pardoning and showing mercy" (Collect Tenth Sunday after Pent.).

[43] "The more numerous and more malignant the sins He pardons, and the more unworthy and miserable the sinners pardoned by Him, the more brightly shines forth His glory. . . . So God Himself,

merciful and loving God, Who, by reason of some small merit, the result of virtue not altogether lost, turns on the most abandoned and desperate sinners, in the hour of death, a gracious and benignant countenance, wakes them to a heartfelt repentance for having sinned against their compassionate Creator and Redeemer, and thus gains them admission to pardon, and, after satisfaction made to His justice in Purgatory, entrance into the Kingdom of Heaven.[44] And if St. Francis de Sales,[45] judging from the point of view above taken, saw reason to hope that the grace of final repentance was awarded to Henry IV. of France, notwithstanding that he died without confession, immediately after receiving his death-

---

most merciful and most loving towards sinners, and moved by some past merit or other, often shows Himself so benignant and amiable to the most desperate offenders when death is near, that they mourn from their inmost heart for having ever offended so good a Creator and Redeemer. Thus repenting, they are doubtless fitted to attain salvation ; and, after having purged away their sins in Purgatory, are translated to the eternal joys of Heaven" (Blosii, Opera 1606, *Canon vitæ spiritualis*, cap. ii.)

[44] St. Gertrude once hearing from a zealous preacher that it was impossible for any one to be saved who did not experience so much love for God as should excite to repentance, bethought herself that, if so, very few were saved, as, according to her notion, the fear of Hell rather than the love of God, was to most persons at the hour of death the motive for repentance. To her thought, the voice of our Lord replied : "When I behold any one in his last agony who has sometimes regarded Me with love, or who, for My sake, has done some works of good, I show Myself to him in so loving a guise that his inmost heart is pierced with sorrow for having offended Me, and repenting, he is saved" (*Vita S. Gertrud*. del Campacci Venez. 1748, p. 2; Ammæstr. 68, p. 219; e del Lansperio, lib. iii. cap. xxxix. G. 2).

[45] "Which makes me hope that the sweet and merciful providence of the Heavenly Father may have insensibly instilled into the great royal heart at the moment of dissolution the contrition necessary for a happy death" (*Epit. Spir*. liv. v. epist. lxxix. tom. i. p. 582, Edit. 1647 ; ou tom. i. p. 538, lett. cxcv. Edit. 1817).

wound, and moreover had been guilty, as trustworthy chroniclers relate, of divers acts of apostasy, and was to the last fettered by his amours, and notorious for unchastity; how much more reason have we for hoping well of those whose fall is due to frailty and to the extreme pressure of suffering?

Ignorant, then, as we are of what passes between God and the sinner who is at his last hour, and is still conscious, but can make no sign, and more utter strangers still to those countless means of saving sinners which, as St. Gregory the Great remarks, are stored up in the depths of God's mercy, how can we presume to say that these weak and erring human creatures are eternally damned?[46]

Blosius, however, warns us against the ingratitude of being led on to sin by the consideration of the goodness of God, a mistake which has proved fatal to many who have abused the Divine bounty. Remember that though God has promised to pardon the sinner whenever he repents, He has not promised, as St. Gregory says, to afford him always time for repentance.[47]

---

[46] "Let no one dare to despair of his neighbour's salvation, for he knows not the riches of the mercies of God" (Hom. *In Evang. Matt.* xx. tom. ii. p. 110).

[47] "He Who has promised pardon to the penitent, has not promised a to-morrow to the sinner" (Hom. xiii. *In Evang.*)

CHAPTER IX.

Discussion of the question, whether the justice of God is not another name for severity.

FIRST DIFFICULTY.—The mercy of God is celebrated far and near, *but He is also infinitely just; and although His mercy is also infinite, yet it is exercised within certain limits.* Who can guarantee that in our case these limits have not been reached, and all that now remains for us is to experience the rigours of His justice? How can we, in this state of uncertainty, feel that assured hope enjoined on us by God under pain of damnation?

Answer.—In the first place, it is most perfectly true that God is as just as He is merciful, for all His Divine perfections are alike infinite. But it must be remarked that justice in God does not necessarily imply, as some suppose, severity in His punishment of sin. On the contrary, the justice of God, as defined by Bergier in his Encyclopædic Dictionary, is that perfection in the Deity whereby He fulfils the promise made to His creatures of rewarding virtue and punishing vice.[1]

---

[1] "The justice of man consists in rendering to every man his due. It supposes the existence of mutual rights and duties; and its supreme law prohibits the infliction of mutual wrong, and enjoins mutual aid in case of need. The idea of justice embodied in this description is inapplicable to the justice of God. Owing us nothing, not even existence, He created us. Everything we possess we owe to His gratuitous liberality. Therefore we have no right to expect anything from Him except as the result of His own promise. His infinite perfections furnish the only laws that bind Him" (Bergier, *Dict. Encyclop.*).

Jesus Christ illustrates the justice of God by the parable of the talents,[2] and shows it to consist in a fair estimate of the good and bad use we make of His gifts, with a view to our reward and punishment;[3] for God having so promised, cannot prove false to His word.[4] Hence with good reason might St. Paul promise himself that, because he had to deal with a just Judge, he was sure of being crowned in reward for all his toils and sufferings.[5]

And although God, in order that we may learn to regard Him as the punisher of vice as well as the rewarder of virtue, has employed threats[6] as well as promises, still as He is not obliged to act when He threatens, but can, notwithstanding any threat of punishment, pardon when He pleases; and as He exercises His mercy without being compelled thereto by any obligation,[7] we may well conclude with St. Augustine[8] that God is both good and just. His goodness leads Him to save where there is no merit; His justice prevents Him from condemning where there is no guilt. "If He ever punishes the sinner, He does so," says Bergier,[9] "for the sake of mankind in general." For this reason, when the Marcionites and the Manicheans objected to the cruelty which God displayed in His

---

[2] St. Matt. xxv. 14—31; St. Luke xix. 12—27.

[3] "I come quickly to render to every man according to his works" (Apoc. xxii. 12).

[4] "God is not as a man that He should lie, nor as the son of man that He should be changed" (Numb. xxiii. 19).

[5] "There is laid up for me a crown of justice, which the Lord the just Judge shall render to me in that day" (2 Tim. iv. 8).

[6] *Vide* St. Augustine, *Contr. duas Ep. Pelag.* lib. iv. cap. vi. n. 16.

[7] "I will have mercy on whom I will, and I will be merciful to whom it shall please Me" (Exodus xxxiii. 19; Rom. ix. 15).

[8] *Contr. Julian*, lib. iii. cap. xviii. n. 35.

[9] L.c.

Solution of Difficulties. 153

punishment of sinners in the early ages of the world, the holy Fathers replied, that but for God's action in that particular, the world had ceased to be habitable, and all the good who were in it would have become the prey of the uncontrolled machinations of the wicked.

The mercy of God may be looked on as an extra weight thrown into the scales of Divine justice; it inclines the balance on the side which leads God in His infinite goodness to bear with us, to pity us, to preserve us from the commission of sin, and to pardon sin committed. Well may we exclaim, in all the fulness of gratitude, "He hath not dealt with us according to our sins;"[10] for as a father compassionates the errors of his children, so God, Who knows our frailty, has compassion on us; and being rich in mercy—yea, the Father of mercies—will not fail, even when He chastens, to act the part of a loving Father, Whose delight is to show His tender pity[11] for the child of His affections.

In the second place, although there are bounds set to the exercise even of the infinite mercy of God, as well as of all His other perfections, those bounds are the duration of man's life and the obduracy of man's heart, and have no existence on the part of God. While life remains, provided we ourselves be not obdurate,[12] God is at hand to exercise mercy in the pardon of sin. He tells us by the mouth of the Prophet Ezechiel[13] that He will not hold our sins in remembrance, but that on what

---

[10] Psalm cii. 10.

[11] "As a father hath compassion on his children, so hath the Lord compassion, . . . for He knoweth our frame" (Psalm cii. 13). "Rich in mercy" (Ephes. ii. 4). "Father of mercies" (2 Cor. i. 3). "When Thou art angry Thou wilt remember mercy" (Habac. iii. 2). "His tender mercies are over all His works" (Psalm cxliv. 9).

[12] See part i. Tesoro x.

[13] "The wickedness of the wicked shall not hurt him in what day soever he shall turn from his wickedness" (Ezech. xxxiii. 12).

day soever we turn to Him with a contrite heart, our sins shall no longer hurt us, and that our merits, which had been dead, shall revive again.[14]

SECOND DIFFICULTY.—Granted that the Lord is our compassionate Father; but what avails His being so, when He is at the same time our severe and inexorable Judge?

Answer.—Let it be admitted that Jesus Christ is also our Judge; yet to suppose that He delights in exhibiting His infinite majesty and power in the chastisement of His unhappy creatures, is to form an idea of His nature which would be a wrong and insult even in the case of an earthly judge. The office of judge is not incompatible with the possession of a kind and compassionate heart; and although a judge may never allow himself to be biassed in favour of injustice, no rule forbids that he should be more pleased when he has to satisfy the requirements of justice by acquitting the innocent or rewarding well-doers, than when he has to do so by punishing the guilty. In the first case, he is but seconding the promptings of his heart; in the latter he obeys the imperative dictates of right order and the requirement of the common weal.

Now who can deny the attributes of mercy and goodness to our Divine Judge? In order to realize their extent we will imagine a case. Suppose, for instance, an entire nation risen in unprovoked rebellion against its lawful sovereign, whom we shall further suppose to be beyond the reach of fear, and to have ample means at hand to crush and punish his rebellious subjects. The sovereign happens to be a just man, and cannot therefore allow impunity to rebellion, whilst on the other

---

[14] "I will restore to you the years which the locusts have eaten" (Joel ii. 25).

Solution of Difficulties. 155

hand he is so good and full of pity for his rebellious subjects, that his whole thought is how to pardon them without compromising the claims of justice. Under these circumstances, having a son equally tender-hearted and compassionate with himself, he appoints that son as judge between him and them.

The son, on the one hand actuated by filial reverence and love, naturally wishes to exact atonement for rebellion; but on the other, being filled with pity and compassion for the rebels, he is desirous to shield them from punishment.

In this conflict of justice with pity, what course does he adopt? He offers to take the place of the guilty, and to make ample, aye, more than ample satisfaction to his father's offended majesty, by submitting in person to all the punishment due to the rebels. The king, his father, who also loves the rebels tenderly, accepts the mediation and offer of his son, permits his arrest and imprisonment, and yields him up a prey to every ignominy and a death of pain. Meanwhile the son cheerfully accepts his fate, and does not shrink either from torments, disgrace, or death; whereby he hopes to gain immunity for the rebels, and shield them from the consequence of their misdeeds. He enters into a compact with his father, which provides that any rebel who really regrets his crime and sues for pardon in the son's name, shall be restored to his status and all his rights as they existed before his rebellion. He establishes everywhere throughout the kingdom tribunals of mercy for the convenience of such rebels as may wish to return to their allegiance, and gives all his judges the amplest powers of pardoning criminals. He pledges himself to forget all offences when pardoned, and promises pardon not alone to those who have rebelled but once, but to those who have done so after repeated pardons. In fact, he assigns no limit to the number, and no exception to the nature, of the crimes open to pardon. One injunction alone forms an exception: he warns them against the deliberate abuse of his great clemency; for he gives them full notice that if the ministers of his justice should ever take them red-handed in rebellion, or before—having had the opportunity—they had pleaded guilty to one of his judges, all his pity should cease, and condign punishment overtake them. But so anxious is he to prevent any one being taken by surprise before he could appeal to one of his tribunals, that he warns all that they shall be liable to arrest by the ministers of his justice when they least expect it, and he earnestly exhorts them, one and all, to have the judge's certificate of pardon and justification ready [15] for such a contingency. He even ventures his person among the rebels, and goes about among them, urging them to seek refuge in his tribunals. "Turn ye, turn ye," he keeps on crying, "why, oh, why will ye die?"[16] "Oh, return and live!" In fine, he leaves no means untried whereby he may cause their restoration to favour with his father, and save them from the punishment which their own obstinacy might bring upon them.

Say, could you possibly do a greater injustice to such a judge as we have here portrayed than to describe him as a fit object for terror—one with a disposition so prone to rigour as to take delight in the punishment of the guilty? If threats of severity against obstinacy occur occasionally in his warnings to the rebels, are they not to be accepted as so many proofs of his desire to reclaim them, and to spare himself the pain of punishing their

---

[15] "At what hour you think not, the Son of Man will come. Be ye therefore prepared" (St. Luke xii. 40).
[16] "Turn ye, . . . why should ye die" (Ezech. xxxiii. 11). "Return ye and live" (xviii. 32).

perverseness? Had not these rebels every reason for confidence, and an assured hope of pardon, if they only appealed to the judges he had set over them, and, with sincere expressions of regret for their crimes, sued for remission of the penalties they had incurred?

Is not the foregoing case our own? But oh, how much greater is the charity of our Divine Judge and Redeemer, Jesus Christ, than that of the supposed judge! Oh! what motives of confidence are here to be found!

The Father made over all judgment on the Son, because He was the Son of Man,[17] as Jesus Christ was pleased to style Himself; in other words, the Father placed our cause in His hands, because, being flesh of our flesh, and bone of our bone, He would, as our Head, have compassion on us, His members. In fact, we possess in Him, as St. Paul says,[18] a High Priest Who has learned to compassionate our infirmities from personal experience of all our woes, with the single exception of sin. Hence He gave Himself[19] to death for our redemption not once alone; for, not content with paying all our debts, and cancelling the sentence of death deservedly pronounced against us,[20] He in addition instituted the Sacrifice of the Mass, in which He continually offers Himself on our behalf, laying bare before His Eternal Father the Wounds He suffered for us and the Blood He shed. Thus does He, before assuming

---

[17] "For neither doth the Father judge any man, but hath given all judgment to the Son, . . . because He is the Son of Man" (St. John v. 22, 27).

[18] "For we have not a High Priest who cannot have compassion on our infirmities; but one tempted in all things like as we are, without sin" (Heb. iv. 15).

[19] "He was offered because it was His own will" (Isaias liii. 7).

[20] "Blotting out the handwriting of the decree that was against us, . . . fastening it to the Cross" (Coloss. ii. 14).

the office of Judge, act the part of advocate, and of an advocate full of zeal and ardour in our cause.[21]

What, then, have we to say in view of all the Divine goodness? If God be for us, who will be against us? Who will accuse us? God Himself justifies us, and who will dare to condemn us? Will it be that Jesus Who died for us, and still intercedes on our behalf?[22] He Who decided on remaining with us, and on becoming, through the august Sacrament of the Altar, one substance with us, to be our help in life and our stay in death, to be our shield against the infernal enemy, and a foretaste to us and pledge of eternal glory?[23]

No doubt He declares that He will act with stern and inexorable justice when the time comes for sitting in judgment; but His threat touches not those who during life repent of their sins and sue to Him for pardon. To such as these He has promised, as we observed before, not only pardon, but oblivion of their sins. His threats of severity are for those alone who continue obstinately in a career of iniquity and wrest the goodness of God to the purpose of multiplying their offences against Him.

To conclude. Let the obstinate sinner fear God, as his Judge, and let him cease from sinning and be converted. But let the man who has offended in the past, and has repented, or is disposed to mourn over and abandon sin, turn to Him as to a Father, and he shall find Him all goodness in His readiness to grant pardon.[24]

[21] "My little children, . . . if any man sin, we have an advocate with the Father, Jesus Christ the just" (1 St. John ii. 1).

[22] "What shall we say then to these things?" If God be for us, who is against us? . . . Who shall accuse against the elect of God? God that justifieth. Who is he that shall condemn? Christ Jesus that died, . . . Who also maketh intercession for us" (Rom. viii. 31—34).

[23] "A pledge is given us of eternal glory" (Antiph. in Office SS. Sacram.).

[24] "He is bountiful to forgive" (Isaias lv. 7).

THIRD DIFFICULTY.—Are there not several texts of Scripture which prove the severity of God? Are we not told that "His justice will take precedence of His mercy:"[25] Does not Jesus Christ Himself declare that "on the dread Day of Judgment His first object will be to punish the wicked, and his next to reward the just."[26] Does He not proclaim Himself "a terrible God, a God of revenge," in a word "a God so jealous that He will visit the sins of those fathers who break His commandments upon their children to the third and fourth generations?"[27] With all this before our our eyes how can we believe Him to be a God of goodness and mercy?

Answer.—With regard to the first text taken from the Royal Prophet, it is to be observed that the inspired writer is not there speaking of any existing fact; he is describing a great future event; His phrase is "shall walk," which he uses in his description of the Messias Who was to come, as may be plainly seen by the summary at the heading of the Psalm that furnishes the quotation. This summary epitomizes the Psalm as descriptive of the coming of Christ, to bring peace and salvation to men, and the body of the Psalm is a prayer to God for mercy on His people for the sake of the future Messias.

By reference to the Scriptures, we moreover find that the first act of God in regard to angels and men was one of bounty, namely, their creation; further on in

---

[25] "Justice shall walk before Him" (Psalm lxxxiv. 14).

[26] "In the time of the harvest I will say to the reapers, Gather up first the cockle . . . to burn; but the wheat gather ye into My barn" (St. Matt. xiii. 30).

[27] "O Lord God, great and terrible" (Daniel ix. 4). "The Lord, the God of revenge" (Psalm xciii. 1). "I am a jealous God, visiting the iniquity of the fathers upon their children unto the third and fourth generations to them that hate Me" (Deut. v. 9; Bergier, *Dict. Encyclop.* tom. vi. p. 193).

Genesis we find [28] that, though He cursed the serpent, and poured out His wrath upon him, in the case of man He abstained (as Bergier, quoting from St. John Chrysostom,[29] remarks), from all invective and reproach, and in all His words dealt gently with him, even when He was passing sentence on him as his judge for the sin he had committed. On that occasion, before dooming him to this life of wretchedness, and expelling him from Paradise, God spoke words of comfort, and consolation, and boundless mercy, in His promise of a Divine Redeemer; for in this sense the sacred interpreters all understand the words addressed by the Lord to the serpent: "She shall crush thy head." [30]

With regard to the second text above cited, it is to be observed that when our Lord bids the reapers gather up the cockle, which is afterwards to be burned, He merely symbolizes the separation, which the angels will be directed to effect on the Day of Judgment, of the bad from the good.[31] But when actual judgment comes to be foreshadowed in the parable, we find the award of Heaven is made in favour of the just before sentence of punishment is pronounced against the wicked." [32]

Again, in the parable of the talents, we find the two faithful servants are rewarded before the idle one is condemned. [33]

---

[28] "Because thou hast done this thing, thou art accursed" (Gen. iii. 14).

[29] Hom. *In Epist. ad Rom.*

[30] Genesis iii. 14, 15.

[31] "The angels shall go out, and shall separate the wicked from among the just" (St. Matt. xiii. 49).

[32] "Come, ye blessed of my Father, possess the Kingdom" (St. Matt. xxv. 34). "Depart from Me, you cursed, into everlasting fire" (41).

[33] St. Matt. xxv. 21, 23.

It follows that, if we are to draw any inference from these two parables, it must be one corroborative, not of God's justice—in the sense of severity—but of His mercy.

No doubt God is sometimes, as Bergier remarks, designated in Holy Writ by such epithets as "jealous, terrible, and the avenger," but they only mark the necessity that existed of rousing the fears and stimulating the reverence of a people so stiff-necked and prone to idolatry as the Hebrews. In order to preserve them from idolatry, God tells them that He will not tolerate their offering to false gods the worship due to Him alone.

In the first place we must observe with St. Augustine, that when God threatened to visit the sin of idolatry on the third and forth generations, he had in view temporal and not eternal, punishment. "We read in Scripture," says the Saint, "instances of men being struck dead for the sins of others, but not a single instance of a man being damned on account of another."[34]

In the second place it imports no violation of Divine justice that the innocent and the guilty should be involved in one common calamity. The calamity affords the innocent an opportunity of earning by patience their promised reward, and cannot be looked on in the light of a chastisement. If we consider how immensely the reward transcends the suffering by which the reward has been won, we shall be apt to think that God conferred on them a very great favour in affording them an opportunity of acquiring so much merit. This consideration fully explains the answer given by St. Augustine to the Manicheans, when they found fault with the action of God in this particular: "Know you," replies the holy Doctor, "what reward God

---

[34] L. i. *Contra adver. Legis et Prophet.* cap. xvi. n. 30.

has prepared for those who have been taken from life that their death may be a warning and corrective to the living."[35]

Besides, we should bear in mind that, if God threatens to visit the third and fourth generations with punishment, He at the same time promises mercy to those who keep His commandments unto a thousand generations.[36]

No doubt our Lord shows Himself a terrible God in punishing obstinate and incorrigible sinners, but He is tender and compassionate to the sinner who, bowing to His punishment, humbles himself, turns to his God, repents and amends. How often in Holy Writ has our Lord reiterated His promise to be ever true to these conditions of His mercy.

In regard to the last text above cited, it is to be observed, that our Lord is therein styled "the God of revenge," in order, according to St. Paul, to mark how decidedly God set His face against man's wreaking vengeance on his fellow man, and that He reserved to Himself all matters relating to retribution. For man is too liable to be deceived, and to be made the sport of passion, to be intrusted with the settling in his own case the limits of equity and justice. If, then, the Lord at any time assumes the dread office of revenger, He does so most unwillingly, and only after many trials of His patience, as was well exemplified in the tears shed by Jesus Christ whilst He was prophesying the destruction of Jerusalem. God is as slow

---

[35] L. ii. *Contra Faust.* capp. lxxviii. lxxix. ; lib. ii. *Contra adver. Legis et Prophet.* cap. xi. n. 35. See Bergier *Dict. Encyclop.* "Justice."

[36] "Showing mercy unto many thousands to them that love Me and keep My commandments" (Deut. v. 10). "And mercy to them that love Him and to them that keep His commandments unto a thousand generations" (vii. 9).

to punish as He is prompt to reward; witness how promptly He promised Paradise to the penitent thief, but abstained from all allusion to the impenitent one. In a word, we have God's own assurance, that when He is in the very act of chastising, He is ready to pardon and bless him whom He punishes provided the latter turn to Him with a contrite heart.[37]

And if the Lord bade the Israelites to tremble before Him in the sanctuary, it wàs to enforce the warning and command, as contained in Leviticus, against the introduction of superstitious practices and idolatry within that holy place, and not for the purpose of introducing terror as an element into His worship.[38]

FOURTH DIFFICULTY.—Did not our Divine Redeemer pronounce an extremely severe sentence on the slothful servant in the Gospel,[39] not because he did evil, but because he failed to do good; the only fault alleged against him being that he omitted, from fear of being made accountable, to trade with the talent which had been intrusted to him, and so returned it intact to his master? And have not we, who are stationary and make no progress in virtue, good reason to anticipate a like sentence in our own case? Or should we not rather say, a harsher sentence, seeing that St. Bernard[40] has declared that not to advance is to recede, and that therefore we shall be deemed, not slothful, but wicked servants, and shall be punished accordingly.

---

[37] "When His wrath shall be kindled in a short time, blessed are all they that trust in Him" (Psalm ii. 13). "No one hath hoped in the Lord, and hath been confounded" (Ecclus. ii. 11).

[38] Bergier, *Table de la Divine Miséric.* pp. 136, 137.

[39] "The unprofitable servant cast ye out into exterior darkness" (St. Matt. xxv. 30).

[40] "Not to advance in the way of salvation is to retrograde" (St. Bern. Serm. xi. *Pour le jour de la Purification*).

Answer.—It is far from true that our Lord pronounced sentence against the slothful servant, irrespective of any evil laid to his charge; for the Royal Psalmist [41] long ago classed among evil-doers those who are deaf to the calls of duty; and it was for a total neglect of the duty imposed upon him that this slothful servant was punished. That duty, imposed upon him by his master, was to trade with the talent placed in his hands, [42] a duty he not only neglected, but perversely ran counter to. For, instead of trading with it, and turning it to the best account in his power, as he was ordered to do, he hid it in the earth. He was therefore rightfully punished for his neglect; which, besides slothfulness, involved the crime [43] of disobedience towards one who had ample authority to impose on him the duty.

Neither is there any reason for our being downhearted because we happen to be stationary and make no progress in virtue; for though we ought, according to the admonition in Ecclesiastes, [44] to strive with all earnestness to become saints, we may be assured that if we do all in our power to avoid sin, God will not fail, as He Himself assures us, [45] to reward us with glory. For, we must remember, it is impossible to avoid sin without obeying the commandments of God, and the precepts of the Church, and consequently without the constant performance of good works.

In order to avoid sin, we are bound for instance to

[41] "But such as turn aside into bonds, the Lord shall lead out with the workers of iniquity" (Psalm cxxiv. 5).
[42] "Trade till I come" (St. Luke xix. 13).
[43] "Wicked and slothful servant" (St. Matt. xxv. 26).
[44] "Whatever thy hand is able to do, do it earnestly" (Eccles. ix. 10).
[45] "He that could have transgressed and hath not transgressed, and could do evil things and hath not done them; therefore are his goods established in the Lord" (Ecclus. xxxi. 10).

the following duties. We must believe and hope in God; we must love and honour Him, and reverence His holy name. We must keep holy the festivals of the Church, as prescribed; we must respect and obey superiors, pardon injuries, restrain anger, abstain from unlawful indulgence — and to that end, mortify the senses—recur to God in temptation, and at once reject its promptings; we must repress the inordinate love of money, and therefore be just in all dealings; we must not injure our neighbour in his reputation, nor rashly judge evil of him, and therefore we should be prompt in urging excuses for him; we must sometimes suffer to avoid falsehood, &c.; we must confess and communicate, fast and abstain on the days prescribed by the Church; we must attend to the education of our children, and watch over the welfare of subordinates, &c.

Let us not imagine that God makes no account of the discharge of the foregoing duties because they are matters of obligation; for as our Lord punishes their infringement, or neglect, He rewards their punctual observance. In point of fact, He Himself has assured us that there is no other condition attached to the attainment of salvation but the observance of the commandments.[46] Nay more, we may without any difficulty acquire continually increasing store of merit; for if we strive to live in the grace of God, and offer up all our actions to His honour, the very duties which we discharge in fulfilment of the obligations of our state of life, become so many helps to Heaven, and bring an increase of merit, grace, and glory.

The observation of St. Bernard, that "he that does not advance recedes," is therefore quite borne out; for whoever does all he can to avoid sin, must necessarily

---

[46] "If thou wilt enter into life, keep the commandments" (St. Matt. xix. 17).

do some good, and doing some good must, more or less, go forward always; whilst on the other hand whoever does no good must necessarily neglect his duties, and consequently disobey the commandments of God and the Church, and therefore, doing no good, he must necessarily sin and retrograde.

Whoever, therefore, performs to the best of his ability the duties of his state of life, and, should he fall into sin, endeavours to rise again through repentance, never ceases to advance; and, like the traveller who, stumbling on his path, quickly recovers himself, and proceeds onwards to his journey's end, he will reach in good time his heavenly country.

Should we even have been hitherto strangers to good, what is there, says Bergier,[47] to hinder us now, now at the very moment we are reading these lines, from making a fervent resolution from henceforward to work out our salvation in earnest, and to make amends for past neglect by zeal and energy in the future? Thus may we hope to achieve a reward as great as if we had made an earlier commencement; and, like the labourers who had been summoned to work by the Lord of the vineyard at the eleventh hour, with them receive the full hire stipulated for an entire day.[48]

FIFTH DIFFICULTY.—There is no middle path to Heaven. As is commonly said, there are only two roads thither, Innocence and Penance. Unfortunately we have long since lost the one, and have never entered on the other. How, then, can we hope to be saved?[49]

Answer.—It is true that either innocence or penance is necessary to salvation; but we should distinguish

[47] *Table. de la Miser. Divin.* p. 27.
[48] St. Matt. xx. 2.
[49] "Except you do penance, you shall all likewise perish (St. Luke xiii. 5).

between the penance which is absolutely necessary to salvation and that which is relatively so, that is to say, such as being merely useful, is of counsel alone.

The first penance absolutely necessary consists in participation with due dispositions in the Sacrament of Baptism and in the Sacrament of Confession. Of these two, the first, as Jesus Christ Himself has said,[50] is necessary for all; the second, that of Confession is necessary, as laid down by the Council of Trent,[51] for all who, after having received the Sacrament of Baptism, have mortally sinned.

The second penance absolutely necessary for salvation to all adults, consists in the conquest of our passions, evil inclinations, and temptations, in a word, in the observance of the commandments of God and the Church. So taught our Lord when, replying to the young man's question how he was to be saved, He said: "If thou wilt enter into life, keep the commandments."[52]

Observe, however, that any one prevented by serious indisposition from observing the commandments of the Church, who patiently bears its infliction for God's sake, shall derive great merit from this indisposition, and make it stand in the place of penance.

The third penance absolutely necessary for salvation, and common to all alike, inasmuch as it is the lot of all to suffer and endure, consists in bearing with patience the innumerable ills and afflictions that wait on this

---

[50] "Unless a man be born again of water and the Holy Ghost, he cannot enter into the Kingdom of God" (St. John iii. 5).

[51] "The Sacrament of Penance is necessary to salvation for those who have fallen after Baptism, just as Baptism is necessary for the unregenerate" (Sess. xiv. cap. v.).

[52] "What good shall I do that I may have life everlasting? If thou wilt enter into life, keep the commandments" (St. Matt. xix. 16, 17).

life of misery.[53] These, if with God's grace we bear them resignedly, will become a never-failing well-spring of merit, and help to discharge the debt due by us in Purgatory. Behold, then, how, by making a virtue of necessity, we may practise a penance of sovereign efficacy.

The fourth penance absolutely necessary for salvation, but applicable only to Religious, consists in the observance of the evangelical counsels, to which are to be added the rules of each community.

Finally comes the penance which consists in mortification. Mortification is either of the powers of the soul, and then it is called interior; or of the senses, and then it is called exterior. Again mortification, both interior and exterior, is divisible into ordinary and extraordinary mortification. Ordinary mortification either is, in individual cases, essential to abstinence from sin, and in such instances is absolutely necessary for salvation; or it is imposed at the tribunal of penance; whence, as being essential to the integrity of the Sacrament of Confession, it is absolutely necessary for salvation. Observe, however, that with regard to this last kind, if the penance first intended is found to be beset by unusual difficulties, no prudent confessor, upon being so informed, would fail to change it for one more practicable. Extraordinary mortification consists wholly in works of supererogation, and is a penance not absolutely necessary for salvation. It has been practised by many of the saints, and is an admirable means of advancing to sanctity and perfection. But its use should be altogether regulated by our spiritual directors.

All are not capable of extraordinary, especially ex-

---

[53] "That which is at present momentary and light of our tribulation . . . worketh for us an eternal weight of glory" (2 Cor. iv. 17).

terior mortifications, and our Lord therefore does not require them from all. In fact they should be used only by persons acting under advice, and with a due regard to their state and condition of life.

Let each one of us, then, in his own sphere strive to practise all necessary penance according to the distinction now pointed out; be assured that whoever does so, although he have forfeited all claim to innocence, shall not be excluded from the ranks of the penitent.

SIXTH DIFFICULTY.—We are told that the anchorites of old, notwithstanding their holy and penitential lives, were liable from time to time, during their course of existence, and also at the approach of death, to fits of the deepest gloom and despondency. One case especially, that of the holy anchorite Stephen, is related by St. John Climacus, who mentions how, after a life of the greatest holiness, when death at last was at hand, he was unable to give any answer to the accusations of the devil, and expired without a word, leaving the attendant monks in the utmost alarm for themselves, and uncertainty as to his salvation. If such things could be in the case of these holy anchorites, what answer shall we be able to give in a similar emergency? How much more reason have we, who in life have been utter strangers to the penitential austerities practised by them, to tremble before the approach of death?

Answer.—The first observation which occurs with regard to the case of the solitary Stephen as related by St. John Climacus, is that the Saint mentions, not that he was condemned to Hell, but that the issue of his eternal salvation was left in doubt.

In the next place, it is impossible to suppose that one, who had led so holy a life as this solitary, was condemned for sins, which, he said, he had nothing to set against but the mercy of God. For the sins he had been guilty of were committed either at some previous period of his life, or at the last hour of existence when confession was impossible. If they had been committed at some previous period, he had duly confessed them, or omitted them through forgetfulness without any fault on his part—and this considering the holiness of his life, we cannot reasonably attribute to him—in either of which cases he might be morally sure of pardon; [54] or if he had committed them in the last moments of existence, when confession was no longer possible, he had it in his power to ask God's pardon with a contrite heart, a pardon which, according to the Divine promise (in a previous page cited from Ezechiel)[55] he should infallibly have obtained. Besides, it would be doing great injustice to St. John Climacus to say that he threw the slightest doubt on this promise from God; so far was he from doing so, that he concludes his narrative of events with this closing ejaculation: "Woe is me! where, oh where was Ezechiel's voice to confront the tempter with the words, 'in whatever hour the sinner shall be contrite, he shall be saved?' he was unable to give with truth any such answer to his enemy."

As to the expressions of doubt respecting the salvation of the solitary, and of alarm for their own, attributed to the monks, it must be remembered that some of them proclaimed their entire confidence in God, and blessed Him; whilst others, yielding to the inferior part of their nature, gave way to feelings of alarm and doubt, which they should have resisted as so many temptations to mistrust the mercy of God, and as sins against the Christian's hope.

[54] See *ante*, cap. ii. diff. 3.
[55] "The wickedness of the wicked shall not hurt Him, in what day soever he shall turn from his wickedness" (Ezech. xxxiii. 12).

Solution of Difficulties. 171

SEVENTH DIFFICULTY.—Can there be a better proof of the severe and inexorable character of our Judge than the following language of Royal David, himself so great a saint: "Thy judgments," he exclaims, "are a great deep. I am afraid of Thy judgments."[56] How can we poor sinners ever enjoy any respite from fear, or any hope of justification, when this holy Prophet, this model of penitence fashioned after God's own heart, trembled at the thought that no man living shall be justified in the sight of that God,[57] in Whose eyes the very saints themselves and their best actions are but uncleanness and an abomination,[58] as the Prophet Isaias said of himself. Nay, more, that God, Who, as holy Job says, finds wickedness in His very angels?[59]

Answer.—If the judgments of God are dark and inscrutable as the depths of the seas, they are also, as the same Royal Psalmist says elsewhere,[60] infinitely just. They have, moreover, the special characteristic, as St. James informs us for our consolation,[61] of having for their end to exhibit in our regard rather the treasures of God's mercy than the rigours of His justice. Although, therefore, when, like the Royal Prophet, we are involved in sin we may well, and should, like him, be afraid of God's judgments; yet when we have also, like the same Prophet, wept over our sin, we may, like him too, draw hope, confidence, and consolation, rather than fear, from their consideration. For in God's judgments, the royal

---

[56] "Thy judgments are a great deep" (Psalm xxxv. 7). "I am afraid of Thy judgments" (Psalm cxviii. 120).

[57] "In Thy sight no man living shall be justified" (Psalm cxlii. 2).

[58] "And we are all become as one unclean, and all our justices like the rag of a menstruous woman" (Isaias lxiv. 6).

[59] "In His angels He found wickedness" (Job iv. 18).

[60] "Thy judgments are equity" (Psalm cxviii. 75).

[61] "Mercy exalteth itself above judgment" (St. James ii. 13).

penitent tells us, he found comfort, and delight, and sweetness beyond honey and the honeycomb, and hope, help, and confidence.[62]

It is undoubtedly true, that "no man living shall be justified in the sight of God;" but this means that, apart from the merits of Jesus Christ, no man shall be so justified, for our Lord Himself says, that without Him we can do nothing.[63] We are, however, assured,[64] that Jesus Christ is our justice, sanctification, and redemption; and therefore we may appeal with confidence to the Eternal Father in Heaven; and, all unworthy as we are in ourselves, plead in our justification what His Divine Son has done and suffered for us.[65]

As for the text from Isaias above cited, St. Jerome, for its better apprehension, reads it in connection with the verse immediately preceding.[66] Read by this light, and the added commentary of Cornelius à Lapide, the two verses may be thus expounded: "We, who are steeped in sin, cannot look for salvation except through the mercy of the Lord God; for as to us Jews, we are guilty, unclean, and filthy in the eyes of God and men."

The words "our justices" in the text, far from meaning the best actions of the Prophet, are interpreted by the holy Fathers and sacred expositors, on the authority

---

[62] "I remembered, O Lord, Thy judgments of old, and I was comforted" (Psalm cxviii. 52). "For Thy judgments are delightful" (39). "The judgments of the Lord . . . are sweeter than honey and the honeycomb" (Psalm xviii. 10, 11). "Thy judgments shall help me" (Psalm cxviii. 175). "In Thy words I have hoped exceedingly" (43).

[63] "Without Me you can do nothing" (St. John xv. 5).

[64] "Christ Jesus . . . is made unto us . . . justice and sanctification and redemption" (1 Cor. i. 30).

[65] "Look on the face of Thy Christ" (Psalm lxxxiii. 10).

[66] "Behold thou art angry and we have sinned; in them we have been always, and we shall be saved" (Isaias lxiv. 5).

of St. Paul, to mean the various purifications and rites enjoined by the Old Law;[67] which, says the illustrious St. Jerome, are, when contrasted with the purity of the Gospel, deemed by the Prophet to be mere uncleanness. Cornelius à Lapide assigns as a reason for the Prophet's denunication, that after these rites and purifications had been abolished by Christ, they should become dead, and even putrid.[68] Hence he concludes that in this text the Prophet does not allude either to himself or to Christians, but, as is evident from the fifth verse above referred to, to those wicked Jews, who, steeped in sin, had recourse to rites and purifications for the purpose of expiation.

If, however, we hold that the words "our justices" mean good works, the text in question presents nothing repugnant to our sense of right. For if we consider the works, even of the saints, simply in themselves, and apart from any virtue derived from the merits of Jesus Christ, they wear an aspect of uncleanness when contrasted with such good works as are illuminated by grace, and seen through the light reflected from their supernatural object. For nothing, with merely the light of common day upon it, can stand comparison with that which glows with supernatural light.

Again, even the best works of the saints may be deemed imperfect, if considered either with reference to absolute perfection, to which none but the acts of the Blessed Virgin—whose works were unalloyed by the shadow of imperfection—was attained; as when com-

---

[67] "Justifications of the divine service" in the Old Law (Heb. ix. 1).

[68] "'All our justices are as the rag of a menstruous woman.' This is a phrase put into the mouth of the wicked Jews, who sought for the expiation and justification of their sins in their purification and sin-offerings" (Cornelius à Lapide).

pared with the infinite perfection of God, or the works of Jesus Christ, to which belongs infinite merit.

We must, however, be on our guard against supposing that this text gives any sanction to the idea that the works of the saints are unclean by reason of any inherent taint of sin; a heresy broached by Luther and Calvin, and condemned as such by Leo X. and the Council of Trent.[69]

Lastly as to the text from Job; it does not mean to imply that God now finds wickedness in His angels; for the slightest imperfection,[70] not to say wickedness, cannot exist in Heaven; all the text means to say is this: if the rebel angels, when they fell away from God, could not disguise from the Searcher of hearts their wickedness, which existed only in thought, how much less able shall we be to hide from His all-seeing eye the depravity of our works, done in the light of day?

As for the rest, the Blessed Angela of Foligno, having, by means of a more than common light shed upon her mental vision, become acquainted with the bounty of the judgments of God, ever after found as much delight in saying, by Thy judgments, as in saying, by Thy Passion, O Lord deliver me![71]

Let then, says St. Augustine,[72] the fear of death, and

---

[69] Sess. vi. cap. xvi. can. vii. *De Justif.* "In every good work the just man sins" (Luther, *In Assert.* xxxi. 32). "In his good work the just man sins mortally" (*Ibid.* art. 36). Calvin says that the works of the just are mere iniquity" (*Instit.* l. ii. cap. i. § 9). "Should any one assert that the just man sins even venially, not to say mortally, in a good work, so as to deserve eternal punishment therefore, and is only not damned because God does not impute it to him unto damnation, let him be anathema" (Sess. vi. cap. xvi. can. xxv. *De Justif.*).

[70] "There shall not enter it anything defiled" (Apoc. xxi. 27).

[71] *In Vita,* vis. 5.

[72] *De Doct. Christi,* lib. i. cap. xv.

consequently of the Divine judgments, be upon those who are unhappily conscious of being in a state of mortal sin, for Divine Justice would be constrained to condemn them, being in this state, to Hell. Let their fear, however, be a profitable fear, and such as shall lead to a change of life, that will dissipate all fear. But he who, from the testimony of his own conscience, is morally certain of being in a state of grace, may be also morally certain of justification before the tribunal of God.

EIGHTH DIFFICULTY.—If the judgments of God be not in reality terrible, how comes it that saints like St. Mary Magdalen dei Pazzi and St. Hilarion found death so fraught with terror?

Answer.—How many, on the other hand, have exhibited the most lively demonstrations of delight at the approach of death? how many saints, as may be seen in the story of their lives, passed so tranquilly from this world to the next, that death seemed in them but a sleep?

St. Liguori[73] relates that a certain religious of the Society of Jesus, and Gerard, brother of St. Bernard, laughed and sang through excessive joy at dying.

Suarez, when dying, said he never knew how sweet a thing it was to die; and St. Louis[74] expired with the words, "we depart with joy."

Sister Mary of the Cross, a nun of the Order of Discalced Carmelites,[75] was so overjoyed at the prospect of death, that she said, if she were cured, grief for her very recovery would cause her death.

Theodora Landi died laughing, and saying: "My Christ's I was, and I am, and I shall be."

---

[73] *Sposa de G. C.* cap. ii. § 20, cap. xxi.
[74] "We go rejoicing" (see his Life).
[75] In the Life of St. Teresa, lib. ii. cap. xiv. See Rogacci, part ii. pp. 502, seq.

Sister Mary of Venice, when she saw death approaching, called out in ecstasy: "To Heaven! to Heaven!"

A certain matron, Fulvia Segardi,[76] summoned musicians to her death-bed, to usher in with their sweetest strains her new and more auspicious birth.

Sister Antonina of St. Hyacinth, a Dominican nun,[77] in answer to some one who expressed surprise at her joy in dying, said: "Ah! God summons me from my long-endured prison to His eternal glory, and have I not good reason to rejoice."

Cardinal Baronius, when commending his departing soul to God, exclaimed: "Courage! behold now is the time for joy and gladness: let us die!"

In like manner two other Cardinals, more than ordinarily overjoyed at the approach of death, died, one exclaiming that he was going to his nuptials, the other singing the Psalm of David, "The Lord is my light and my salvation, whom shall I fear?"[78] and whilst repeating the words, "One thing I have asked of the Lord," &c., his spirit flew rejoicing to the abode of God.

A religious of the Society of Jesus, named Joseph Scamacca, when dying was heard to say, "Oh, joy!" and on being asked whether he was about to die in the assured hope of salvation, by way of reply said, "Have I been serving Mahomet, think you, that I should now doubt of the goodness of my Lord?" And so of many others, whose history is recorded by Father Rogacci.[79]

Indeed, a slight examination will show us that the deaths of almost all the saints were distinguished by peace and serenity. And a similar observation may be extended to the deaths of all who live good Christian lives.

[76] Rho. *Hist. virt.* lib. ii. cap. iii.
[77] Le Blanc, *In Psalm.* cxxi. art. i.
[78] Psalm xxvi. 1.
[79] See Rogacci, part ii. p. 504.

And if we read a few instances, like the two mentioned above, of saints showing alarm at the approach of death, the alarm may have arisen in these exceptional cases from the withdrawal by God of sensible consolations, whereby these saints have been made to experience the anguish of feeling themselves forsaken during their mortal agony, similar to that felt by Jesus Christ when He uttered a cry of desolation during His dereliction on the Cross.[80] If this be a true solution, we may be sure that God at the same time imparted to these saints abundant graces, all the stronger for not being sensible, to enable them to bear in the manner most meritorious to themselves the anguish attendant on the fear of being forsaken by God. We may learn, however, from the lives of the saints, that God visits the souls that are dear to Him with such a trial as this much more frequently during the course of life than at the hour of death.

On the other hand, these fears may be temptations to want of confidence proceeding from the devil, permitted by God for the greater profit of His servants, in order to obtain their entire purification and consequent exemption from Purgatory, or a greater increase of merits, as St. Gregory the Great remarks, through their exercise of those virtues most opposed to the temptation. St. Gregory adds, that those servants of God are never unduly depressed thereby, and that they are always reanimated and restored to joy by the thought of their eternal reward.[81]

---

[80] "My God, My God, why hast Thou forsaken Me?" (St. Matt. xxvii. 46).

[81] "When dissolution is at hand, the soul even of the just man is oftentimes troubled by fear of retribution, because the souls of the just are frequently purged from some lighter stains by alarm at death. Generally, however, before they have quitted the body they exult in the thought of their eternal reward, and thus they at once pay an old debt, and reap the joy of new fruition" (*Mor.* lib. xxiv. cap. xviii.).

This fear and wavering, therefore, have their rise in the inferior portion of the soul, and never in the superior, which invariably casts them off. This was the case with St. Hilarion, who, after having served God in the desert by a long life of austere penance, was suddenly overtaken at the approach of death by fears and doubts. They were, however, at once shaken off by the superior powers of his soul, and, taking fresh courage, he cried out, "Go forth, go forth, my soul, of what art thou afraid? Nearly seventy years hast thou served God in the desert, and art thou now afraid of death?"

As though the Saint had said, "Go forth, my soul, and fear not. Hadst thou served a tyrant, or some miserable, thankless creature who cared nothing for thee or for thy good, and had as little power as will to serve thee in thy utmost need, thou mightest have cause to fear that thy labours and service would be scattered to the winds; but thou hast served the God Who made thee, a God Who loves thee as His child, and died on a Cross for thy salvation—the Almighty God; and art thou afraid to appear before Him? Oh, go forth, for thou hast nothing to be afraid of, but everything to hope from His bounty."

In point of fact, this holy anchorite, as St. Jerome tells us, being sick unto death, and remembering that he had no heir, made a will full of fun and humour. He thereby bequeathed all his property and possessions to his disciple Esichius; all which property and possessions consisted of a copy of the Gospel, a tunic of sackcloth, a cowl, and an old overcoat. Moreover, he distinctly told every person that visited him in his last sickness that he was about to go to his Lord. From the foregoing it is evident that, far from fearing death, it was to him an object of joy, and that he urged his soul to hasten her departure from the body that she might be the sooner united to her Creator.

As to the case of St. Mary Magdalen dei Pazzi, her desolation of spirit at the hour of death need cause us no surprise. For we learn from St. Liguori [82] that the Saint herself, after five years of unmitigated sufferings from the extreme of bodily pain, and from temptations of various kinds, prayed God never again to afford her any sensible consolations; and when life was drawing to a close, she expressed a wish [83] that, as Christ had died on the Cross, forsaken and unconsoled, so she might expire upon the hard and naked cross of unalloyed suffering. And her desire was granted; for speaking, a few hours before she passed away, with the utmost peace and tranquillity, she declared that up to that moment her spirit was still a prey to desolation, unrelieved by a gleam of joy, and returned thanks to God on that account in an act of resignation to the following effect: "I am satisfied with whatever pleases Him, and I thank Him for it; and I now again sacrifice to Him all spiritual joys and comforts in exchange for my salvation."

Had these two Saints entertained any serious diffidence as to their ultimate salvation, they would have been wanting in that heroic hope which is the distinctive characteristic of saints.

NINTH DIFFICULTY.—Who may secure us from the fate of the youth of whom it stands recorded that upon the very night of the day on which he had committed a sin of unchastity, he was surprised by death and condemned to Hell?

What becomes of the vaunted goodness of God, set forth in His protestation, made through Ezechiel, that

[82] *Opere Spirit.* p. 353. Edit. Torino, 1826.
[83] See her Life by Puccini. Venice, 1739.

He awaited the return of sinners in order to show them mercy; if He awaits them, so to say, on the threshold, and strikes them dead and damns them on the very first act of sin? Did He not act so towards the rebel angels, whom He cast headlong into Hell while they were in the very act of sinning, no time being allowed for repentance or for pardon? Who knows but that, if God had waited for them, they would have been converted?

Answer.—The apprehension of consenting to sin, and of being, like the unhappy youth, surprised by death while in that state, should teach us to be careful to avoid evil occasions, to be diligent in frequenting the sacraments, and prompt in having recourse to God, as the best preservatives against temptation. Above all, his example warns us not to rest for the briefest space under the guilt of mortal sin; but, if we have the misfortune to incur it, to fly at once to the feet of God and sue for the grace of repentance and pardon, before we are overtaken by death and destruction. Remember that St. Gregory tells us [84] that, although God has promised to pardon the sinner who repents, He has not promised him time for repentance; and that Jesus Christ Himself warns us [85] that death will come when we least expect it. And although the Almighty, in order that the ordinary course of His providence in the government of the world may not be interfered with, permits such casualties, He takes care that they, and the consequent misfortune of individuals, shall redound to the public good, in the lesson they teach men in general not to abuse time while it is still theirs, or the patience of a merciful God.

Moreover, we ought to be on our guard against indi-

---

[84] "He who has promised pardon to the sinner, has not promised him a to-morrow to sue for it" (Hom. xii. *In Evang.* sub fin.).

[85] "Be you ready, for at what hour you think not the Son of Man will come" (St. Luke xii. 40).

rectly attempting to detract from the goodness of God by compassion for sinning men. For although it is a terrible thing for the sinner to be cut off in his sins, yet (as we before observed in discussing the meaning of the text, "for three crimes of Damascus," &c.[86]) St. Ambrose —and with him agrees St. Bernard—says that the prolongation of their lives would involve far more cruelty to the sinners in question, inasmuch as their protracted obstinacy in sin would add to the horrors of their damnation.[87] And if, with St. John Chrysostom, we put the supposition that, had God given them a respite they might have repented and been converted, we may adopt the answer given by the holy Doctor to his own surmise, namely, that had such a result been possible, God would have postponed their death.[88] In fact, continues St. Chrysostom, seriously to believe in the possibility of such a supposition being realized would be a grievous wrong to the goodness of that God Who, in all He did and suffered, ordered everything with a view to our salvation. This being considered, it is impossible to conceive that if by the exercise of a little forbearance on the part of God the sinner could be won round to make himself acceptable in the Divine sight, our Lord would not allow him to remain longer in life. If God bears with those who never cease offending Him, would He not, *à fortiori*, spare the lives of those who, if allowed to survive, would be converted?

[86] Ch. ii. diffic. 7.

[87] "Death is bitter to the wicked, but life is still bitterer than death; for it is a more grievous burthen to live in sin, than to die therein; for the wicked increases his sin in proportion as his life is prolonged; if he dies, he ceases to sin" (St. Bernard, Lib. *De Bono Mortis*, cap. i.; Serm. *De fallacia præs. vitæ*).

[88] "But perhaps he would have changed his life, had he lived: but God would not have carried him off, if in case of his living he would have so changed" (Epist. ad Philip. cap. ii.; Serm. viii. in fin.; *Digress. Moral.* tom. iv.).

The Saint continues the same strain in his 69th Homily addressed to the people of Antioch, saying that whenever a man dies in sin he at least is prevented from sinning any more, and that if God foresaw that a prolongation of life would have led to his conversion, He would have extended it.[89]

The same observations apply to the case of the rebel angels. According to Cornelius à Lapide, supported by St. Gregory of Nyssa, and the opinion of the Fathers and of learned commentators on 2 St. Peter ii. 4, these angels were allowed a space, doubtless very short, for repentance, and, not availing themselves of it, were hurled headlong into Hell. And although the spectacle thus presented is very terrible, still we have herein room to admire the goodness of God. For the Lord either foresaw, as St. Gregory remarked about sinners generally, that they would never be converted, or He did not. If He foresaw it, then, by causing their perdition, He prevented an augmentation of their sufferings as the result of a multiplication of sins; if He did not, then by their immediate perdition God prevented the possible fall of many others of the angelic hosts, who might have been seduced by the fact of so great a scandal being allowed to continue amongst them; nay, by this means He probably confirmed the others in grace, and rendered them thenceforward incapable of sinning.

[89] "The evils are ended, if the evil-doer be departed; nor would God, if He foresaw his repentance, remove him before he had repented" (In fin. tom. v. p. 1115. Edit. Paris, 1614. *Vide* Sarasa, *Ars semper gaudendi*, tract. xv. par. 1, p. 287. See also in this book ch. viii. diffic. 4, at the end).

CHAPTER X.

Discussion on the question, whether the generality of preachers and ascetic writers, concur in the foregoing interpretation of the texts herein selected for exposition.

THE DIFFICULTY.—How comes it then that so many preachers and ascetic writers of celebrity, comprising in their number several saints, have put so stern an interpretation on the foregoing texts, and used them for the purpose rather of inspiring hearers and readers with terror, than of consoling them with considerations suggestive of hope and pardon?

Answer.—In the first place, if we examine the texts thus used, we shall find, generally speaking, that originally they conveyed merely the historical statement of the temporal evils inflicted on or threatened against certain sinners by God; and that afterwards they were applied by celebrated preachers and writers, in a figurative sense, to describe eternal and spiritual torments, denounced against sinners in general.[1] It is also right to observe

[1] In this way Father Segneri applies the text from Judges xvi. 20, "The Lord had departed from," &c., which primarily expresses merely the loss of his strength on the part of Samson by the act of God; also the text from 1 Kings xvi. 1, "How long wilt thou mourn for Saul, whom I have rejected from reigning over Israel," which merely referred to the rejection of Saul by God from the throne of His earthly kingdom; and again, the text from Jeremias vi. 30, "Call them reprobate silver, for the Lord hath rejected them;" and another from Lamentations iv. 22, "Thy iniquity is accomplished, O daughter of Sion; He will no more carry thee away into captivity," which passages announce the calamities with

that these texts, so far from being, in their original sense, menaces of spiritual evils, actually imported great spiritual good conferred by God on sinners;[2] for such temporal chastisements as they indicated, had no reference to eternal damnation, but were intended to promote their conversion,[3] and to save them from falling into further evils, and ultimately into the pains of Hell.

In the second place it is to be observed, that whenever these preachers and writers apply the harsh method of interpretation to these texts—moved thereto by their anxiety to touch the hearts of sinners, and terrify them into repentance—and when for that purpose they adopt the figurative sense, or when they use certain oratorical exaggerations permissible[4] under the circumstances,

---

which Jeremias threatens the priests and elders of Jerusalem, as well as the destruction of that city itself (see vol. ii. Serm. ii. n. 6, p. 97, and vol. i. v. 12 of the Psalm l. n. 2, c. 4, pp. 472, 473). St. Liguori makes a similar use of the text from Numbers xiv. 22, 23, "They have tempted me now ten times, and shall not see the land," which merely referred to the exclusion of the Israelites from the promised land; and of the text from Genesis xv. 16, "For as yet the iniquities of the Amorrhites are not at the full," which merely announced the postponement of the Amorrhites' castigation, in consequence of their not having yet filled the measure of their iniquity and of the before-mentioned rejection of Saul (Discourses 15, n. 4). These and other passages of Scripture, which in their original meaning, relate to temporal misfortunes and abandonment, have thus by these Fathers been applied in the figurative sense of menaces to obstinate sinners of final reprobation and eternal punishment.

[2] For it is a token of great goodness when sinners are not suffered to go on in their ways for a long time, but are presently punished (2 Mach. vi. 13).

[3] Not as being for the destruction but the correction of our nation (2 Mach. vi. 12).

[4] Instances of such exaggerations are not unfrequently found even in Holy Writ, as, for instance, where Elias says (3 Kings xix. 14), "The children of Israel have forsaken thy covenant, ... and *I alone* am left," although at that very time seven thousand remained faithful, as appears by his subsequently adding (18), "I will leave me seven

Solution of Difficulties. 185

they do not stop there. For, by dwelling on milder views, and by introducing more consoling topics, in the same, or a succeeding discourse, they invariably modify and mitigate the harshness of their previous exposition,[5]

thousand men in Israel whose knees have not been bowed to Baal." Again, Esdras, upon hearing of the introduction of strange women into Israel, gave way to such paroxysms of grief, tearing his hair and rending his garment, abandoning himself to the most profound melancholy, and uttering such piteous cries to the Lord, as to lead to the inference that the greater part if not the whole of the people had been led astray. These were his words: "Art thou angry with us unto destruction, not to leave us a remnant to be saved" (1 Esdras ix. 14), whereas at the very time he was speaking, out of "all the multitudes ... forty-two thousand three hundred and sixty, besides their men-servants and women-servants" (ii. 64), there were only one hundred and fourteen really guilty (see further, Esdras x. from verse 18 to 43 inclusive).

[5] In point of fact, Father Segneri subsequently modifies his previous application of the text referring to Saul (Sermon xxi. tom. ii. n. 5, p. 188, col. 2); and in like manner, in explaining "You shall seek Me ... and shall die in your sins" (Sermon xi. tom. ii. p. 91), and the text "Be not without fear about sin forgiven" (tom. i. v. 12 of Psalm l. p. 743), he uses the words "No one in the world shall ever persuade me that I can be damned against my own will" (Sermon xxxi. tom. ii. n. 1. p. 278). And his language is more unmistakeable further on: "The necessary helps for attaining eternal life are never withheld even from the most wicked" (*Ibid.* p. 281, n. 5. col. 2; tom. i. v. 2, *Del Sal*, 50, 719, especially where he treats of renovations and the proportionate increase of gifts, helps, and habits). See, finally, tom. ii. pred. 32, n. 2, page 228; col. 1, n. 4, p. 290; col. 1 e 2, n. 6, p. 292; col. 1. n. 7, p. 293; col. 1 e 2, n. 10, p. 296, col. 2, where, addressing his words directly to Jesus Christ, he thus concludes his Sermon xxxii.: "Thou shouldst not have placed me in this office if Thou didst not intend me to extol Thy mercies in the most munificent spirit. From this pulpit I will not alone promise Thy pardon to all who seek it, but that Thou wilt admit them to Thy friendship; and that, as Thou now givest them grace to rise, Thou wilt in the future give them the power to persevere; I will tell them that 'He who hath begun a good work in you will perfect it'" (Philip. i. 6). He also (tom. ii. pred. 16, p. 140, n. 3, col. in fine, pred. 26, p. 235, n. 6, col. 2; tom. i. v. 9, *Del Sal*, 50, p. 733) modifies his observations on fear

following in this the prudent advice given by St. Liguori, namely to leave a door open to the sinner whereby to enter whenever he wishes to repent.[6]

(tom ii. pred. 7, p. 61, second. part. n. 7. col. 1), saying with the Angelical Doctor, that perfect charity, according to St. John (1 Ep. iv. 18), casteth out the fear of punishment and increaseth the fear of guilt, which is a filial fear; all which he explains in its proper place. St. Liguori also endeavours to strike terror into the sinner in his Sermon xi. (§ 10), and then administers comfort and consolation by his reflections on the Passion of our Lord, saying (p. 123) that Jesus Christ had made Himself our advocate with His Father, in order to obtain mercy for us when we should unhappily fall into sin (1 St. John ii. 1). In his Sermon xxxii. (§ 11, p. 3) and his Tract on "the great instrument of prayer" (p. ii. cap. ii. pp. 143, 146, and 149). he expresses sentiments agreeing with the Venerable Cardinal Bellarmine, in his work on Nature and Grace (c. xviii.), and with St. Thomas, and essentially modifying his previously expressed opinions about the sinner's abandonment alluded to in our previous note; and he distinctly lays it down that "there is no sinner so lost to grace and utterly forsaken, that has not the power, if he so wills, to subdue his own obstinacy and yield himself a convert under the influence of that same grace" (1 *Sent. Dist.* 48, q. 1. a. 3 ad 2). He concludes with this extract from Soto: "I am more certain . . . nay, I believe that all the holy doctors were always most certain that no one ever was utterly abandoned in this mortal life" (*Ibid.* p. 152). The Blessed Leonard of Port Maurice (tom. ii. pp. 30, 31, 33, 35, and 283; tom. iii. pp. 146 seq.) utters the most awful denunciations against sinners, and apparently leaves them without a hope of pardon; but he either at once, as in tom. ii. p. 35, or at the end of the same, or in the course of some subsequent sermon, administers consolation and dwells on soothing topics, as may be seen by comparing tom. ii. p. 30 with tom. iii. p. 170; tom. ii. p. 35 in its several passages one with the other and with tom. iii. pp. 171 and 312; tom. iii. p. 146 and following with tom. iii. pp. 299, 300, and 301; in which last he represents Jesus Christ saying to St. Peter, "Hearken, Peter: should sinners come to thee in proper dispositions, make no delay to grant them pardon; never refuse it." And he goes so far as to say that "it is an impiety and blasphemy to say, 'Who knows if Jesus Christ will pardon me?'"

[6] In sermons which have for their object to inspire terror, let the preacher beware of leading his hearers to despair of salvation or of amendment of life. Let him invariably, before bringing his discourse

In the third place, and lastly, we must consider all the circumstances of time, place, and people in the midst of whom these preachers and writers spoke and wrote.

As to the times, then: they lived at a period when unbelievers and freethinkers had not yet learned to turn those texts, by putting a harsh interpretation upon them, to their own sinister purposes. No effort had yet been made to cast discredit on religion or to blaspheme God by accusing Him of injustice and tyranny and of being so cruel by nature as to take pleasure in the sufferings of His creatures; no deliberate attempts to destroy the faith of the weak by exciting hatred against God, and the religion which inculcates belief. At that period no danger attended on the rigorous interpretation of those texts, which on the other hand might be adopted with advantage in addressing the faithful, in arousing the energies of the lethargic and subduing the obstinacy of the hardened sinner. In our times, however, that method cannot be adopted with the same profitable results, and perhaps not without considerable danger to souls.

Next, with regard to circumstances of time and place. It is an acute observation of Bergier[7] that the principal ascetic writers passed their lives in large and populous cities, where the greatest corruption of morals usually prevails, and the attempt is made to gloss over vice

---

to a close, open a door for every, even the most abandoned, sinner, through which he may pass on the road to amendment. Let him encourage the sinner to trust in the merits of Jesus Christ and in the intercession of His Blessed Mother, and to have recourse in prayer to these two sheet-anchors of the Christian's hopes. Let the preacher then frequently and urgently inculcate in his sermons the practice of prayer as the only sure means of obtaining the graces necessary for salvation (Selva, *Di Materie Predicabili*: Avvertisementi, &c. tom. i. n. 6. p. 3).

[7] *Tabl. de la Miser. Divin.* p. 5.

or make it excusable, if not justifiable. In the midst of such surroundings their zeal, as sagacious as it was indefatigable, would endeavour to stem the swollen torrent of wickedness, to awake the torpid, and excite all to repentance by an appeal to the sentiment of fear.

Indeed, St. John Chrysostom, among others, as we before remarked, preached at Antioch to a congregation composed of disorderly Catholics, whose lives were corrupted by contact with all manner of unbelieving Gentiles, who formed the staple of its numerous population.

Blessed Leonard of Port Maurice preached in Corsica at a period of great disorder caused by the spirit of faction. To such a pitch did this spirit rise, that in the churches where he gave his missions, especially in the Church of Castel d'Acqua, the several bands of partisans attended his sermons, armed to the teeth and under the guidance of their respective leaders, ready to fly at each other's throats on the slightest provocation.[8]

St. Francis, St. Liguori, and Father Segneri preached in Italy to Italians at a time when that people were more inclined to presumption than despair; and ere yet there was any danger of abuse, as we before observed, from the sneers of the scoffer.

We should not therefore be surprised that these illustrious preachers and writers, particularly Blessed Leonard, actuated by the motives here stated, thought it their duty, in times gone by, to appeal to the fears of the obdurate sinners to whom their discourses were addressed. The chief hope of conversion and submission to the holy law of God for that stiff-necked generation lay in their dread of everlasting punishment and the severity of the Divine justice.

[8] *Vita.* Edit. Venezia, 1756, cap. xvi. pp. 208, seq.

CHAPTER XI.

Question considered: Is the method of directing souls by the way of confidence a dangerous one?

THE DIFFICULTY.—The results of adopting the milder system of interpretation with regard to the texts quoted from the Scriptures and the writings of the holy Fathers appear to be as follows: (1) It teaches the faithful that they should get rid of all apprehension; (2) that sinners may live on at ease in sin, since salvation is of such easy attainment through repentance; (3) that no duty devolves on the faithful of doing good to the utmost of their ability, seeing that without anxiously striving after sanctity they can acquire large stores of merit merely by the practice of ordinary mortifications and through their common-place, every-day actions. As the foregoing results are manifestly pernicious, the system, which directs souls rather by the way of trust and confidence than by that of fear, cannot be either good or expedient.

Answer.—In the first place it is not true that the milder method of interpretation counsels the discarding of all fear. For not only does it not meddle with that filial or reverential fear,[1] which consists in a horror of

[1] A certain amount of fear was inseparable from the human nature of Jesus Christ Himself, as was foretold by the Prophet Isaias, when he said, speaking of our Lord, "He shall be filled with the spirit of the fear of the Lord" (Isaias xi. 3). This fear of humble reverence for the Majesty of God showed itself in perfection in Jesus Christ when He humbled Himself to the death of the Cross. This hallowed, calm, and tranquil fear, that makes the soul bow down in worship before the infinite Majesty of God, humble

sin because it offends God, but it leaves untouched that servile fear which consists of the spectre of a sudden and unprovided death and consequent damnation, which ever haunts the conscious sinner.

In point of fact, as we before noted,[2] this fear was ever kept before the eyes of sinners by a constant reference to the saying of St. Gregory, that although the Lord promised pardon to the sinner whensoever he should have recourse to Him, God did not promise the sinner time for repentance. They were therefore exhorted not to deceive themselves with the idea that their future sins would meet with the same immunity as attended them of the past, and warned against an abuse of the Divine mercy, which would of itself draw down the judgment of Heaven.

The lesson to be learned by sinners from this method of interpretation is far indeed removed from any encouragement to fall asleep and perish in their sins from an overweening confidence of easily obtaining pardon. On the contrary, its chief aim is to facilitate the speedy conversion of sinners by removing from their minds the great obstacles of despair and despondency, which arise from exaggerated ideas of the difficulty of obtaining salvation.

"No doubt," observes Bergier,[3] "certain perverse natures may carry their confidence to presumption.

---

herself before His Throne, and abhor sin as the supreme evil, is most befitting in those who are by grace in the greatest security of salvation and are destined to dwell for ever with the Blessed above. Such is the teaching of the Angelical Doctor on the authority of the Royal Prophet, who strongly urges it upon all the just: "The fear of the Lord is holy, enduring for ever and ever" (Psalm xviii. 10). "Fear the Lord all ye His saints" (Psalm xxxiii. 10). See St. Thomas 1, 2, q. 67, ar. 4, et 3 p. q. 7, ar. 6.

[2] Ch. ii. diffi. 6, 7, and ch. ix. diffi. 9.
[3] *Tabl. de Miser. Divin.* p. 10.

Such are the men who abuse the Divine mercy by continuing to sin, and who, because God is good and ever open to the call of mercy, sin against Him without intermission. Most assuredly this very ungrateful conduct would merit condign punishment, and that God should confound hopes so vain and abominable in His eyes.[4] Nevertheless it is of the last consequence that men like these, who are liable at every moment to be overcome by the violence of their passions, should be brought to reflect on God's readiness to pardon."[5] "Oh, yes! Well indeed may His mercy be called infinite," exclaims Cornelius à Lapide with reference to this subject; "with us, poor mortals, the greater our injuries the greater is our anger; but with God the greater His wrongs, the greater becomes his compassion. God[6] saw that our nature, corrupted by the influence of the devil, was overmuch prone to presumption and rashness, and compassionating this phase of our misery, He, for this very reason and in the exercise of boundless mercy, promised us pardon on whatsoever day we should turn to Him with all our heart. By this promise He designed to relieve the despondency of the timid, and their faintheartedness in good works; and to prevent sinners, by obstinacy in sin through despair of pardon, from still further outraging His justice which they failed to comprehend. For, as in human society, the worst malefactors are found to be those who from their first entrance on a course of crime have despaired of pardon,[7] so

---

[4] "Their hope is an abomination" (Job xi. 20).
[5] Bergier, l.c. p. 73.
[6] "He hath seen the presumption of their hearts, that it is wicked: and hath known their end, that it is evil; therefore hath He filled up His mercy in their favour, and hath shown them the way of justice" (Ecclus. xviii. 10, 11. See also Cornelius à Lapide).
[7] Bergier, l.c. pp. 7, 63.

would the sinner who despaired of God's mercy become case-hardened[8] in sin and be apt, as St. Paul says,[9] to sink into the lowest depths of vice.

Add to this, if we are to be deterred from advocating any given course from fear of its giving rise to abuses among men, no truth could any longer be discussed, since there is nothing which the malice of man cannot pervert.

In the third place, though we are able to satisfy the punishment due to our sins by accepting in a penitential spirit the ordinary crosses and afflictions that befall us in this vale of tears, and to lay up a large store of merit by the easy method of offering up our daily actions to God, still the facility thus afforded us for obtaining remission of debt, and for acquiring great store of treasure, ought not to have the effect of making us relax in our efforts to do good, but ought to have quite the contrary result.

When a man has lost his all and is crushed by the weight of debt, how thankfully would he make use of any easy way which presented itself not only of paying his debts and getting rid of importunate creditors, but also of re-establishing his fortunes on a sounder basis? How much more ought the facility for bringing his concerns to a successful issue stimulate the sinner in his exertions not only to satisfy the claims of Divine justice, but, by merits stored up on earth, to gain a rich inheritance, and become, by means of Divine grace and his own will, a saint in Heaven.

Our fervour and diligence in well-doing instead of being relaxed, should therefore be stimulated to still

[8] Where hope is taken away, men glide unchecked into vice.
[9] "Who despairing have given themselves up to lasciviousness unto the working of all uncleanness, unto covetousness" (Ephes. iv. 19).

further efforts by the greatness of the reward, and the facility and certainty of obtaining it.

We may infer from the foregoing that the consequences of engendering in the soul a sweet confidence in God far from being pernicious, are most profitable by their encouragement to well-doing. According to the authority of the Angelical Doctor,[10] it is the characteristic of confidence to render those in whom it is active—the presence of God's grace being presupposed—fervent and energetic, not relaxed and indolent, in the prosecution of good works. The consequences are also most profitable to sinners; for confidence in God gets rid of the incubus of despair, that greatest obstacle to conversion and most powerful incentive to vice.

How indeed could the Apostle have exhorted the faithful to abound in hope,[11] if confidence in God were not in entire conformity with the spirit of that adoption of sons, which is our portion under the law of grace.[12]

Whilst, therefore, as His sons, we ought always to fear to offend God by sin; we ought never to fail to repose in Him, as our Father, that sweet confidence which inspires our hearts with ardent and tender love for His paternal mercy and goodness. Ever bear in mind the saying of St. Peter Chrysologus that God assumed the title of our Father in order to establish the reign of love and not fear in our hearts.[13]

DEO GRATIAS.

[10] "It is the characteristic of hope to work out its own object" (I, 2, q. 40, ar. 8).

[11] "That you may abound in hope" (Rom. xv. 13).

[12] "For you have not received the spirit of bondage again in fear, but you have received the spirit of the adoption of sons, whereby we cry Abba, Father" (Rom. viii. 15).

[13] "Let our innermost heart recognize Him as Father, . . . and let our whole being answer to grace and not to fear; for He Who changed Himself from our Judge into our Father, seeks to be loved not feared" (Serm. lxi. et lxix.).

www.ingramcontent.com/pod-product-compliance
Lightning Source LLC
Chambersburg PA
CBHW020923230426
43666CB00008B/1548